MASTER ● THE
Basics

Second Edition

Paul G. Graves, Ph.D.
Formerly, Professor of German
University of Colorado
at Boulder, Colorado

Henry Strutz, M.A.
Formerly, Associate Professor of Languages
SUNY Technical College at Alfred, New York

BARRON'S

All inquiries should be addressed to:
Barron's Educational Series, Inc.
250 Wireless Boulevard
Hauppauge, New York 11788

Library of Congress Catalog Card No. 95-78260
International Standard Book No. 0-8120-9001-2

Printed in the United States of America

678   8800   9876

Contents

Preface

This book is intended as a handy reference guide for high school and college students as well as for business people. It should also be useful for those who have had some German previously and want to "brush up" their grammar. Most of the grammar terms used probably are already familiar to you. You will find them here again set forth carefully, clearly, concisely. Learning grammar is not an end in itself but a tool for acquiring a language. Grammar, if it is to be the indispensable helpmate of language study, should be presented in a friendly, nonthreatening way. This we have tried to do.

High school or college students need a grammar review to serve them as a condensed, yet comprehensible, supplement to their regular textbooks. In this book they will find those terse definitions and easy-to-grasp explanations that they seek. Business persons, as well as other people who want to reinforce their knowledge of German, should find this book a welcome companion.

For the orderly study of language, a minimum of grammar is essential. Memorizing simple phrases might be barely sufficient for casual travelers who want to impress the natives with their smattering of German. In many instances, though, the natives, in response, will try out their English on the disappointed foreigner. Obviously, even a very short conversational exchange requires a minimal knowledge of grammar to structure a proper German sentence.

It is fortunate that the study of German offers no insuperable problems to the person whose native tongue is English. The two languages, after all, are closely related; many word forms and grammatical constructions can be easily identified.

How to Use This Book

You probably already have some familiarity with German. But even if you are not now studying German in class or have never studied it in the past, you will be able to understand a good part of this book without much difficulty. All the examples offered to explain a grammatical point are translated into English, English that is often closely related to the German in form and meaning. For a quick reference, you can consult the index where you find numbers that are keyed to the particular areas that you want to investigate.

The model sentences that illustrate each rule are meant to encourage you to identify the grammatical structure and to help you to recognize how that structure functions to achieve a particular meaning. Don't let fear of making mistakes inhibit you and keep you from speaking the language. In the end you will learn from your mistakes—and learn to avoid making them. Never miss the opportunity to hear German spoken by Germans—in person, on records, or on the radio. Beware of that feeling of frustration that everybody experiences when learning a new language, or relearning it. In the end, you will feel amply rewarded.

FIND OUT WHAT YOU KNOW

Test Yourself

1. The *ch* in *ich* sounds like the first letter of

   kind ☐
   huge ☐
   chop ☐

2. The *v* in *viel* is the same as the first letter of

   veal ☐
   foal ☐
   will ☐

3. The word *mein* rhymes with

   keen ☐
   mean ☐
   fine ☐

Each of the following three sentences contains one error in spelling, punctuation, or capitalization. Find the error and correct it.

4. Hans ist gern Kuchen. _____

5. Am sonntag kommt er zu uns. _____

6. Er trinkt weil er durstig ist. _____

Form sentences from the following words, starting with the subject.

7. zu Hause / er / bleiben / wird _____

   _____

8. besucht / uns / Eva / hat / gestern _____

   _____

9. Kinder / die / hörte / weinen / ich _____

   _____

**PARTS OF
SPEECH**

Complete the following sentences with the appropriate noun endings.

10. Ich habe viele _____. *(Buch)*

11. Das Jahr hat zwölf _____. *(Monat)*

12. Sie liebt schöne _____. *(Blume)*

3

Complete the sentences below by choosing the correct articles.

13. Wo ist _____ Kind jetzt? *(der, die, das)*

14. Wie heißt die Frau _____ Präsidenten? *(der, des, dem)*

15. Der Mann trägt _____ Hut. *(ein, eine, einen)*

Fill in the adjectives (in parentheses) with their correct endings

16. Er spricht mit der _____ Frau. *(hübsch)*

17. Das ist die _____ Wohnung. *(neu)*

18. Das ist ein _____ Kind. *(gut)*

Complete the following sentences with the appropriate pronouns.

19. Anton, _____ bist ein guter Mensch. (you)

20. Er bringt _____ die Karten. (to us)

21. Ich liebe _____ Mutter. (my)

Fill in the correct verb form in the sentences below.

22. Wann _____ er zurück? *(kommen, present tense)*

23. Wir _____ die ganze Nacht _____. *(arbeiten, present perfect)*

24. Karl _____ einen neuen Job. *(finden, past tense)*

25. Er _____ nach London _____. *(fliegen, future tense)*

26. Wo _____ du heute? *(sein, past tense)*

27. Er _____ Hunger _____. *(haben, present perfect)*

Complete the following sentences by filling in the appropriate German adverbs.

28. Sie ist _____ nett. (always)

29. Er ist _____ krank. (unfortunately)

30. Wir sind _____ fertig. (now)

Fill in the appropriate German preposition in the sentences below.

31. Wir fahren _____ Deutschland. (to)

32. Das Buch ist _____ dem Tisch. (on)

33. Der Brief ist _____ meiner Freundin. (from)

Combine the following sentences by using the conjunctions in the parentheses.

34. Sie sind nicht in Amerika. Sie sind in England. (but)

35. Er spielt Schallplatten. Er studiert. (while)

36. Sie geht nicht auf Urlaub. Sie hat kein Geld. (because)

**SPECIAL
TOPICS**

Give the correct gender for these compound nouns.

37. _____ Vaterland *(der, die, das)*

38. _____ Eisenbahn *(der, die, das)*

39. _____ Tannenbaum *(der, die, das)*

Check the box that corresponds to the appropriate English translation for the following German idiomatic expressions.

40. Er hat Grütze im Kopf.

He is sick. □
He is stupid. □
He is intelligent. □

41. Er hat die Nase voll davon.

He is fed up with it. □
His nose is stuffed. □
He feels great. □

42. Er führt etwas im Schilde.

He is advertising. □
He is up to something. □
He wears a badge. □

43. The number 1 000 000 000 in German is:

eine Million □
eine Milliarde □
eine Billion □

44. One of the sentences below is incorrect. Can you find it?
Amerika wurde im Jahre 1492 entdeckt. ☐
Amerika wurde 1492 entdeckt. ☐
Amerika wurde in 1492 entdeckt. ☐

Write the numerals below in German.

45. 12 = _____

46. 21 = _____

47. 101 = _____

48. 1200 = _____

Write the following times of day in German.

49. 9:30 A.M. _____

50. 5:45 P.M. _____

51. 17:50 _____

Fill in the blanks with the appropriate German word in the following sentences.

52. Herr Schmidt ist am _____ geboren. (February 7, 1952)

53. Der längste Tag des Jahres ist im _____. (June)

54. Die Jahreszeit, die dem Winter folgt, ist der _____. (spring)

Match the words in the left column with their synonyms in the right column.

55. wirklich   unterstützen

56. helfen   passieren

57. geschehen   tatsächlich

Now match the antonyms.

58. dumm   aufhören

59. alt   klug

60. anfangen   neu

Answers

1. huge
2. foal
3. fine
4. ißt
5. Sonntag
6. Er trinkt, weil er durstig ist.
7. Er wird zu Hause bleiben.
8. Eva hat uns gestern besucht.
9. Ich hörte die Kinder weinen.
10. Bücher
11. Monate
12. Blumen
13. das
14. des
15. einen
16. hübschen
17. neue
18. gutes
19. du
20. uns
21. meine
22. kommt
23. haben / gearbeitet
24. fand
25. wird / fliegen
26. warst
27. hat / gehabt
28. immer
29. leider

30. jetzt

31. nach

32. auf

33. von

34. Sie sind nicht in Amerika, sondern in England.

35. Er spielt Schallplatten, während er studiert.

36. Sie geht nicht auf Urlaub, weil sie kein Geld hat.

37. das

38. die

39. der

40. He is intelligent.

41. He is fed up with it.

42. He is up to something.

43. eine Milliarde

44. Amerika wurde in 1492 entdeckt.

45. zwölf

46. einundzwanzig

47. hunderteins

48. zwölfhundert

49. halb zehn morgens, neun Uhr dreißig morgens

50. dreiviertel sechs abends

51. siebzehn Uhr fünfzig Bahnzeit, fünf Uhr fünfzig abends

52. siebenten Februar 1952 (*or*, 7.2.52)

53. Juni

54. Frühling

55. tatsächlich

56. unterstützen

57. passieren

58. klug

59. neu

60. aufhören

Diagnostic Analysis

Section	Question Numbers	Number of Answers	
		Right	Wrong
THE BASICS			
1. Pronunciation	1, 2, 3		
2. Orthography	4, 5, 6		
3. Word Order	7, 8, 9		
PARTS OF SPEECH			
4. Nouns	10, 11, 12		
5. Articles	13. 14. 15		
6. Adjectives	16, 17, 18		
7. Pronouns	19, 20, 21		
8. Verbs	22, 23, 24, 25, 26, 27		
9. Adverbs	28, 29, 30		
10. Prepositions	31, 32, 33		
11. Conjunctions	34, 35, 36		
SPECIAL TOPICS			
12. Word Formation	37, 38, 39		
13. Common Phrases and Idiomatic Expressions	40, 41, 42		
14. Numbers	43, 44, 45, 46, 47, 48		
15. Telling Time	49, 50, 51		
16. Days, Months, Seasons, Dates, Weather	52, 53, 54		
17. Synonyms and Antonyms	55, 56, 57, 58, 59, 60		
TOTAL QUESTIONS:	60		

Use the following scale to see how you did.

58 to 60 right:	*Excellent*
55 to 57 right:	*Very Good*
52 to 54 right:	*Average*
49 to 51 right:	*Below Average*
Fewer than 41 right:	*Unsatisfactory*

A GRAMMAR
BRUSH-UP

The Basics

§1.

Pronunciation

German Letter	Pronunciation
a	ah
b	bay
c	tsay
d	day
e	eh
f	ef
g	gay
h	haa (rhymes with baa)
i	ee (rhymes with sea or see)
j	yut (rhymes with shut)
k	kaa (rhymes with blah)
l	el
m	em
n	en
o	oh (as in no)
p	pay
q	koo
r	err
s	ess
ß	ess-tsett
t	tay
u	oo (rhymes with boo)
v	fow (as in fowl)
w	vay
x	iks (rhymes with six)
y	üpsilon
z	tsett

A German vowel is long if it is followed by a single consonant or by ß (scharfes s) and another vowel, if it is doubled *(aa, ee, oo)*, or if it is followed by a silent *h*.

Alphabet Letters	Sounds	Examples
a	Similar to the *a* sound in "father."	*Gābe* / gift *Strāße* / street

13

Alphabet Letters	Sounds	Examples
e	Similar to the *a* sound in "gate."	*Bēsen* / broom *gēgen* / against
i	Similar to the *i* sound in "mach*i*ne."	*Maschīne* / machine *Berlīn* / Berlin
o	Similar to the *o* sound in "bone."	*Nōt* / need *Brōt* / bread
u	Similar to the *oo* sound in "pool."	*Schūle* / school *gūt* / good
aa	Similar to the *aa* sound in "Saab."	*Haar* / hair *Paar* / pair
ee	Similar to the *a* sound in "hay."	*Tee* / tea *Kaffee* / coffee
oo	Similar to the *oa* sound in "road."	*Bo͞ot* / boat
ah	Similar to the sound in the exclamation "ah!"	*Bāhn* / railroad *Fāhrer* / driver
eh	Similar to the *ai* sound in "fair."	*sēhr* / very *Kēhle* / throat
ih	Similar to the *ea* sound in "team."	*īhm* / to him
oh	Similar to the *o* sound in "tone."	*Lōhn* / wage *Wōhnung* / apartment
uh	Similar to the *e* sound in "grew."	*Kūh* / cow *Hūhn* / chicken

Note: In this chapter only, the symbol ‾ above a vowel (ā) will be used to indicate a long vowel, and the symbol ˇ will be used to indicate a short vowel (ǎ).

- German *ie* is always pronounced like the *ie* in "chief," "priest," or "shield."

A German vowel is short if it is followed by more than one consonant or by a double consonant.

Alphabet Letters	Sounds	Examples
a	Similar to the *o* sound in "don."	*dǎnn* / then *hǎrt* / hard

Alphabet Letters	Sounds	Examples
e	Similar to the *e* sound in "belt."	*Fĕld* / field *hĕll* / clear
i	Similar to the *i* sound of "fins."	*Lĭnse* / lens *Lĭppe* / lip
o	Similar to the *ou* sound in "rough."	*ŏft* / often *Hŏffnung* / hope
u	Similar to the *u* sound in "bull."	*Mŭster* / sample *nŭll* / zero

- The vowel *e* is short when it occurs in the suffixes *-e, -el, -en, -er,* and *-et* and when it appears in the inseparable prefixes *be-, emp, ent-, er-, ge-, ver-,* and *zer-.*

EXAMPLES:

Suffixes

Blumĕ / flower   *Muttĕr* / mother
Apfĕl / apple   *Schwestĕr* / sister
Himmĕl / heaven   *Tochtĕr* / daughter
gehĕn / to go   *Vatĕr* / father

Prefixes and Suffixes

In the following examples, note that the *e* in both the first and last syllables (prefix and suffix) is short.

bĕhandĕln / to treat   *gĕgebĕn* / given
bĕweisĕn / to prove   *gĕschlossĕn* / closed
ĕmpfehlĕn / to recommend   *gĕsegnĕt* / blessed
ĕmpfangĕn / to receive   *vĕrhungĕrn* / to starve
ĕntkommĕn / to escape   *vĕrsprochĕn* / promised
ĕntsagĕn / to renounce   *zĕrfallĕn* / to fall apart
ĕrobĕrn / to conquer   *zĕrreißĕn* / to tear up
erörtĕrn / to discuss

An *umlaut* is the change in a vowel caused by partial assimilation to a succeeding sound. It is indicated by two dots above the vowel.

Umlaut	Sounds	Examples
ä	Pronounced like the short *e, as in* "bet."	*Länder* / lands *mächtig* / strong
ö	Similar to the *u* sound in "further."	*schön* / beautiful *förmlich* / formal
ü	There is no equivalent in English. Similar to the French *u.* Say *ee* with your lips in a whistling position.	*kühn* / bold *für* / for

Diphthongs are pairs of vowels.

Diphthong	Sounds	Examples
au	Identical to the *ou* sound in "ho*u*se."	*Maus* / mouse *Faust* / fist
äu	Identical to the *oi* sound in "s*oi*l."	*Häuser* / houses *Säugling* / infant
eu	Pronounced like *äu*.	*Feuer* / fire *deutsch* / German
ai	Identical to the *i* sound in "p*i*ne."	*Hai* / shark *Mai* / May
ei	Identical to the *y* sound in "tr*y*."	*rein* / clean *breit* / wide

§1.3
CONSONANTS

The following German consonants should cause you no problems.

Alphabet Letters	Sounds	Examples
b	Identical to the *b* sound in "ball," *except* at the end of a syllable and before a consonant (see table below).	*Brücke* / bridge *beide* / both
d	Identical to the *d* sound in "day," *except* at the end of a syllable and before a consonant (see table below).	*dümm* / stupid *dänke* / thanks
f	Identical to the *f* sound in "fat."	*Fähne* / flag *frei* / free
g	Identical to the *g* sound in "gun," *except* at the end of a syllable and before a consonant (see table below).	*Gäst* / guest *Gäbel* / fork
h	Identical to the *h* sound in "here."	*Heim* / home *heiß* / hot
k	Identical to the *k* sound in "kick."	*Kätze* / cat *Köhle* / coal
m	Identical to the *m* sound in "moist."	*Milch* / milk *Männ* / man
n	Identical to the *n* sound in "nut."	*nett* / nice *neu* / new
p	Identical to the *p* sound in "peace."	*Plätz* / place

Alphabet Letters	Sounds	Examples
t	Identical to the *t* sound in "*t*ent."	*Teil* / part *tīef* / deep
x	Identical to the *x* sound in "fo*x*."	*Hĕxe* / witch

The following three consonants are pronounced differently at the end of a syllable or word and before a consonant.

Alphabet Letters	Sounds	Examples
b	Pronounced like *p* in "gra*p*e."	*Grāb* / grave *līeb* / dear
d	Pronounced like *t* in "ren*t*."	*Hănd* / hand *Kīnd* / child
g	Pronounced like *k* in "dar*k*."	*Tāg* / day *săgt* / says

The following consonants are pronounced in different ways, as explained in the table.

Alphabet Letters	Sounds	Examples
c	In foreign words before *e* or *ä*, it is pronounced like *ts* in "ha*ts*."	*Cäsar* / Caesar
j	Identical to the sound of *y* in "*y*es."	*Jāhr* / year *jŭng* / young
l	Should be pronounced with the tip of your tongue against the back surface of your upper front teeth. It should sound like the flat *l* in "William."	*Leute* / people *ălt* / old
qu	Always pronounced *kv*, as in "kvass," a fermented beverage.	*Quălität* / quality *Quărz* / quartz
r	Can be rolled, the way the Scots do it; however, the uvular *r*, similar to the sound of gargling, is preferred.	*reich* / rich *streng* / strict

Alphabet Letters	Sounds	Examples
s	Before a vowel, *s* sounds like the *z* in "zoo." Before a conso- nant or at the end of a word, sounds like the *s* in "hou*s*e."	*Sĭlbe* / syllable *sīeben* / seven *erst* / first *Māus* / mouse
ss, ß*	Both are identical to the sound of *ss* in "gla*ss*."	*Kŭß* / kiss *Küsse* / kisses
v	Identical to the *f* sound in "*f*ather."	*Vŏgel* / bird *vŏll* / full
v	In words of foreign origin, it is identical to the *v* sound in "*v*ery."	*Vĭlla* / villa *Vāse* / vase
w	Identical to the *v* sound in "*v*eal."	*Wĕlt* / world *wō* / where
y	Sounds like the umlaut *ü*. If it occurs as the last vowel in a name, it is sounded like a long *i*.	*tў̆pisch* / typical *Ănnў̄* / Anny
z	Identical to the *ts* sound in "ra*ts*."	*Zeitung* / newspaper *bezăhlen* / to pay

*Note: German practice has been to use *ss* between two short vowels and *ß* everywhere else. Although you will still see the digraph *ß*, it is obsolete, and in time only *ss* will be used.

The following consonant combinations are pronounced in various ways, as explained in the table below.

Alphabet Letters	Sounds	Examples
ch	Identical to the *ch* sound in the name "Ba*ch*" or in the Scottish pronunciation of "lo*ch*"; occurs only after the vowels *a, o, u,* and the diphthong *au*.	*Săche* / thing *dŏch* / however *Tūch* / cloth *Rauch* / smoke
ch	Similar to the exaggerated *h* sound in "*h*umor."	*Bĕcher* / cup *Lĭcht* / light
ch	In certain foreign words of French derivation, pro- nounced like *sh* in "*sh*oe."	*Chănce* / chance *Chĕf* / boss
ch	In certain words of Greek derivation, pronounced like *k* in "*k*eep."	*Chărăkter* / character *Chōr* / choir

Alphabet Letters	Sounds	Examples
chs	Identical to the *x* sound in "fo*x*."	*Ăchse* / axis *Ŏchse* / ox
ck	Identical to the *ck* sound in "bla*ck*."	*Săck* / sack, bag *Blĭck* / look
ph	Identical to the *ph* sound in "*ph*one."	*Phrāse* / phrase *phȳsisch* / physical
sch	Identical to the *sh* sound in "*sh*op."	*Schlāf* / sleep *schwărz* / black
sp	Pronounced like *shp* at the beginning of a word.	*Spĭel* / game *spät* / late
st	Pronounced like *sht* at the beginning of a word.	*Stein* / stone *Stĕrn* / star
th	Identical to the *t* sound in "*t*op."	*Thrōn* / throne *Thēma* / theme

§1.4 STRESS

Boldface type will be used in this section to indicate stressed syllables. There is no written stress in German. Most dictionaries, however, do indicate stress, and it is recommended that you consult the dictionary when in doubt. Here are some general guidelines:

- In simple words of two syllables, the stress is usually on the first syllable.

   EXAMPLES:
   Gabel / fork
   Winter / winter
   Wagen / wagon
   Erde / earth

- In compound nouns that consist of two or three words (see §4.2–3), the main stress is usually on the first word.

   Freizeit / leisure time
   Pelztierzucht / fur farming
   Gartenwerkzeuge / garden tools
   Langstreckenläufer / long-distance runner

- Separable prefixes are stressed most of the time.

  EXAMPLES:
  ableiten / to derive
  ansagen / to announce
  aufstehen / to get up
  aussprechen / to pronounce
  beistimmen / to agree
  einrichten / to arrange
  nachgeben / to give in

- The inseparable prefixes *be-, emp-, ent-, er-, ge-, ver-,* and *zer-* are never stressed.

  bewundern / to admire
  empfehlen / to recommend
  entsprechen / to correspond
  erwerben / to acquire
  gelingen / to succeed
  verarbeiten / to process
  zerreißen / to tear apart

- All nouns ending in *-ei* have the stress on the last syllable.

  Bäckerei / bakery
  Bücherei / library
  Geschrei / shouting
  Konditorei / pastry shop
  Metzgerei / butcher shop
  Wäscherei / laundry

- All verbs ending in *-ieren* have the stress on the next-to-the last syllable.

  EXAMPLES:
  studieren / to study
  trainieren / to train
  telefonieren / to phone

Orthography

Orthography is defined as the art of writing words with the proper letters according to standard usage. It includes topics such as spelling, punctuation, capitalization, and syllabication.

Spelling German correctly is far easier than spelling English. There are no great discrepancies between written and spoken German. Every sound has its own fixed symbol, with but few exceptions—e.g., the silent *h* that serves to lengthen vowels (as in *Lohn* / reward; *mehr* / more). Other than in the combination *ie* (as in *bieten* / to offer), where the *e* serves to lengthen the *i*, *e* is never silent. For "I come" Germans can say or write either *ich komme* or *ich komm*. Written German reflects the spoken language to a higher degree than is the case in English. Mastering German pronunciation (Chapter 1) is a good way to learn German spelling. When in doubt, consult a dictionary.

What we are mainly concerned with in this chapter are those parts of orthography where German deviates from the rules that govern English usage.

2.1 CAPITALIZATION

German conventions on capitalization differ from English in several respects. Here are some guidelines.

- All nouns are capitalized.

  der Bruder / the brother
  der Freund / the friend
  der Mantel / the overcoat
  die Zeitung / the newspaper
  das Messer / the knife
  die Lampen / lamps

- Adjectives and other parts of speech that are used as nouns are capitalized.

  der Dicke / the fat man
  die Kluge / the clever woman
  das Beste / the best (thing, one)
  das Neue / the new (one)
  das Schöne / the beautiful (thing)
  das gewisse Etwas / that certain something

- Adjectives that follow an indefinite pronoun (*jedes, etwas, wenig, viel,* etc.) are capitalized.

  jedes Schlechte / everything bad
  etwas Großes / something big
  wenig Schönes / little that is beautiful
  viel Wichtiges / much that is important

- Pronouns in letters used in the familiar form of address are capitalized.

  *Ich hoffe, daß **Du** das Paket erhalten hast.* / I hope that **you**
    have received the package.

  *Hoffentlich habt **Ihr** Euch bei uns gut amüsiert.* / We hope you
    had a good time at our place

- Pronouns used in the polite form of address are always capitalized.

  *Ich habe **Sie** dort gesehen.* / I have seen **you** there.
  *Wir haben **Ihnen** geschrieben.* / We wrote **you.**
  *Wie geht es **Ihrer** Schwester?* / How is **your** sister?

- The pronoun *ich* (I) is capitalized only if it stands at the beginning of a sentence.

- Adjectives of nationality are not capitalized.

  der deutsche Außenminister / the German foreign minister
  das französische Parfüm / the French perfume

§2.2 Syllabication

Syllabication is the method by which words are divided syllables. It is of interest chiefly at the end of a line in wr communication. New rules for German syllabication ha superseded old ones. It is not necessary for you to worr too much about this issue. Whether you write *Bü-cher* Büch-er (books), the important thing to remember is tha *ch, sch,* and *ß* are single sounds whose components ca not be separated.

- Although the letters *ck* are sounded as a single *k*, they separated into *k-k*. Thus *Bäcker* (baker) becomes *Bäk-*

- The letters *st* are never separated into *s* and *t*.

  EXAMPLES:
  Fen-ster / windows
  höch-ste / highest

BUT
Ge-burts-tag/ birthday
Reichs-tag/ German parliament
Liebes-traum/ dream of love

Note: *Tag* is a word in its own right, a component within a compound word (see §4.2–3), and the *s* belongs to the first word, having been added as a linking or connective letter.

§2.3
PUNCTUATION

German has the same punctuation marks as English, but the rules governing punctuation differ from the English in some respects. Here are some of the main differences:

- In German, a period is used after ordinal numbers.

   EXAMPLES:
   Freitag, den 5. Juli / Friday, July 5
   Ludwig XVI. / Louis XVI

- Independent clauses are set off by commas if they have different subjects and verbs.

   EXAMPLES:
   Paul las, und Edith schlief. / Paul read, and Edith slept.
   BUT
   Paul studierte und hörte dem Radio zu. / Paul studied and listened to the radio.

- Dependent clauses are always set off by commas.

   EXAMPLE:
   Das Hemd, das du trägst, kostet 20 Mark. / The shirt that you're wearing costs 20 marks.

- Any phrase that contains *zu, um zu, ohne zu,* or *anstatt zu,* is set off by a comma.

   Es ist wichtig, ihn mitzunehmen. / It is important to take him along.
   *Sie ging ins Theater, **um** "Hamlet" **zu** sehen.* / She went to the theater to see "Hamlet."

- The last item in a series is *not* set off by a comma.

   Er studierte Englisch, Französisch und Russisch. / He studied English, French, and Russian.

- In German the exclamation mark is used much more frequently than in English. For instance, it is used after a command, an emotive expression, or when beginning a letter

  EXAMPLES:
  Einfahrt verboten! / Do not enter!
  Schön, dich wiederzusehen! / Nice to see you again.
  Das ist großartig! / That's great!
  Lieber Paul! / Dear Paul,

- Nowadays instead of an exclamation mark, a comma is commonly used in the salutation of a letter, in which case the body of the letter begins with a lower-case letter.

  Liebe Freunde, wir freuten uns sehr, von Euch zu hören. / Dear
  Friends, We were very glad to hear from you.

§3.

Word Order

A *sentence* is an organized group of words that express a statement, a question, a command, a wish, or an exclamation. A sentence starts with a capital letter and ends with a period, a question mark, or an exclamation mark.

EXAMPLES:
Kurt liest ein Buch. / Kurt reads a book. (statement)
Liest Kurt ein Buch? / Does Kurt read a book? (question)
Kurt, lies das Buch! / Kurt, read the book! (command)

Sentences consist of two basic parts: a *subject* and a *predicate.*

- A *subject* is the sentence unit that originates the action or the condition indicated by the verb. The subject is the "who" or "what" the sentence is about. It is often the first element in a simple sentence.

EXAMPLES:
Hans spielt die Violine. / Hans plays the violin.
↑

| subject = |
| who plays the violin |

Schnee bedeckt die Stadt. / Snow covers the city.
↑

| subject = |
| what covers the city |

- However, the subject is not always the first element of the sentence. Other parts of speech may precede it.

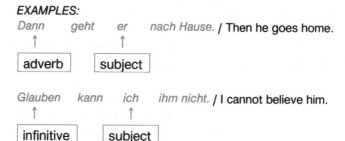

EXAMPLES:
Dann   geht   er   nach Hause. / Then he goes home.
  ↑   ↑

| adverb | | subject |

Glauben   kann   ich   ihm nicht. / I cannot believe him.
  ↑   ↑

| infinitive | | subject |

25

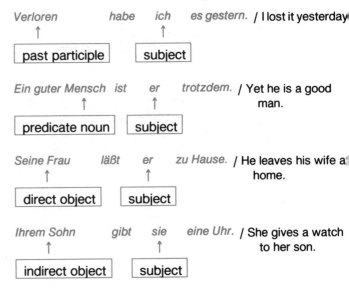

- A *predicate* is that part of the sentence that expresses what is said about the subject.

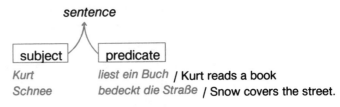

| Kurt | liest ein Buch / Kurt reads a book |
| Schnee | bedeckt die Straße / Snow covers the street. |

- A subject must contain a noun (see Chapter 4) or pronoun (see Chapter 7); a predicate must include a verb (see Chapter 8). The parts of speech that make up the subject and predicate are defined and discussed in Chapters 4 to 11

§3.2
TYPES OF
SENTENCES
ACCORDING
TO FUNCTION

§3.2–1
Affirmative

An *affirmative sentence* states or affirms something in a positive way.

EXAMPLES:
Eva ist Deutsche. / Eva is German.
Dieser kleine Junge spielt Fußball. / This little boy plays footba
Alle unsere Freunde wohnen in München. / All our friends live i
Munich.

The *object* of a sentence is the noun or noun phrase toward which the action of a verb is directed. A *noun phrase* consists of a noun accompanied by an article or adjective. An object can also be a pronoun that takes the place of a noun or a noun phrase.

- There are two types of objects: *direct* and *indirect.* A direct object, or accusative, receives the action of the verb directly. An indirect object, or dative, is the indirect receiver of the verb's action.

> A noun or noun phrase that follows the verb in the accusative is a *direct object.*

EXAMPLE:
Arthur liest die Zeitung. / Arthur reads the newspaper.

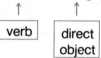

> A noun or noun phrase that follows the verb in the dative (see Chapter 8) is an *indirect object.*

Karl schreibt dem Lehrer. / Karl writes to the teacher.

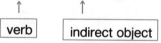

- If both the direct and indirect objects are nouns, the indirect object usually precedes the direct object.

Karl schreibt dem Lehrer einen Brief. / Karl writes a letter to the teacher.

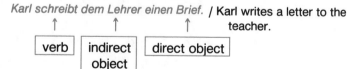

- It is not always necessary to have an object in a sentence.

Uwe schläft. / Uwe is sleeping.
Sie kommt morgen. / She is coming tomorrow.

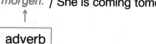

§3.2–2 Negative

A German affirmative sentence can be made into a negative sentence by using the word *nicht* (not).

EXAMPLES:

Affirmative	Negative
Ich will es. / I want it.	*Ich will es nicht.* / I don't want it.
Das ist gut. / That's good.	*Das ist nicht gut.* / That is not good.

Here are some guidelines for the word order of *nicht* in a German sentence.

- *Nicht* precedes a predicate adjective, noun, pronoun, or adverb.

  EXAMPLES:
  Das Wetter war nicht schön. / The weather was not nice.
  Das ist nicht der Mann. / That is not the man.

- *Nicht* precedes a general time expression or a prepositional phrase.

  EXAMPLES:
  Er kam nicht oft. / He did not come often.
  Sie ist nicht zu Hause. / She is not at home.

- *Nicht* precedes past participles and infinitives.

  EXAMPLES:
  Er hat heute nicht gearbeitet. / He did not work today.
  Wir werden dich morgen nicht treffen. / We will not meet you tomorrow.

- *Nicht* precedes separable prefixes.

  EXAMPLES:
  Ich hole dich morgen nicht ab. / I will not pick you up tomorrow.
  Heute kommt er nicht zurück. / He will not come back today.

- *Nicht* precedes the main verb in a dependent clause.

  EXAMPLES:
  Es ist möglich, daß er den Job nicht bekommt. / It is possible that he will not get the job.
  Wir gehen spazieren, wenn es nicht regnet. / We'll go for a walk if it does not rain.

- In a sentence with simple verb forms of the present or past tense, or if the entire sentence unit is to be negated, or for special emphasis, *nicht* can stand at the end of the sentence

EXAMPLES:

Franz gibt Karl das Auto nicht. / Franz will not give Karl the car.
Er gab es ihm nicht. / He did not give it to him.
Peter kommt leider nicht. / Unfortunately, Peter will not come.

- Whenever two persons or objects are to be contrasted, *nicht* can precede any word that it negates, except the conjugated verb.

  Nicht sie, sondern er kam heute zurück. / He, not she, came back today.
  Nicht heute, sondern morgen ist sein Geburtstag. / His birthday is tomorrow, not today.

- German sentences can also be made negative by using forms of *kein*, the negative of the definite article *ein* (see §5.3 and §7.4).

  Affirmative

  Heute brauchen Sie einen Mantel. / You need a coat today.

  Negative

  Heute brauchen Sie keinen Mantel. / You don't need a coat today.

§3.2–3
Interrogative

In an interrogative sentence you ask a question. When you write it, you always put a question mark at the end. As in English, the subject follows the verb.

EXAMPLES:

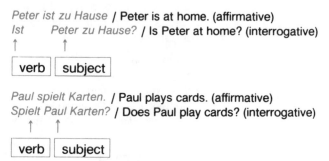

Peter ist zu Hause / Peter is at home. (affirmative)
Ist   Peter zu Hause? / Is Peter at home? (interrogative)
↑   ↑

| verb | subject |

Paul spielt Karten. / Paul plays cards. (affirmative)
Spielt Paul Karten? / Does Paul play cards? (interrogative)
↑   ↑

| verb | subject |

Interrogative sentences can also be formed by using interrogative pronouns or adverbs.

Welchen Film bevorzugen Sie? / Which film do you prefer?
Wie geht's? / How are you?

Use *nicht wahr?* to express the following:

Otto ist sehr nett, nicht wahr? **/** Otto is very nice, isn't he?
Du kommst mit, nicht wahr? **/** You're coming along, aren't you?

§3.3
TYPES OF SENTENCES ACCORDING TO STRUCTURE

§3.3 – 1
Simple

A simple sentence has only one (main) subject and one (main) predicate.

§3.3 – 2
Complex

A complex sentence has one main clause and at least one subordinate, or dependent, clause. It still has a main subject and predicate.

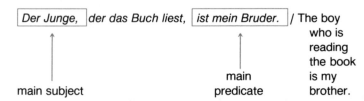

Der Junge, | der das Buch liest, | *ist mein Bruder.* | / The boy who is reading the book is my brother.

main subject

main predicate

Relative Clauses

A *clause* is a group of related words containing a subject and a predicate and is part of the main sentence. A *relative clause* is a subordinate clause introduced by a relative pronoun (see Chapter 7).

EXAMPLES:
Main Sentence
Der Junge ist mein Bruder. / The boy is my brother.
Sentence to Be Changed into a Clause
Der Junge liest das Buch. / The boy is reading the book.

Complex Sentence

Der Junge,	*der das Buch liest,*	*ist mein Bruder.*
↑ main subject	↑ relative clause	↑ main predicate

Please note that in the relative clause on page 30 (introduced by the relative pronoun *der*) the verb moved to the end of the clause.

Temporal Clauses

A *temporal clause* is introduced by a subordinating conjunction. A *conjunction* is a word that joins together sentences, clauses, or other words. The term *temporal* expresses a time relationship.

Als ich nach Hause kam, When I came home,	*war das Essen fertig.* the meal was ready.
temporal clause	main sentence

- As can be seen, the clause introduced by the subordinating conjunction *als* causes the verb *kam* to move to last place. Also, putting the temporal clause first causes inversion — that is, the placement of the verb before its subject in the main sentence.

- However, if we turn the sentence around, there is no inversion:

Das Essen war fertig, The meal was ready	*als ich nach Hause kam.* when I came home.
main sentence	temporal clause

- The rules outlined above also apply to the following examples.

Bevor / before *Bevor er sie besuchte,* Before he visited her, ↑ temporal clause	*kaufte er Blumen.* he bought flowers ↑ main sentence
Nachdem / after *Nachdem ich ihn gegrüßt hatte,* After I had greeted him, ↑ temporal clause	*grüßte er mich.* he greeted me ↑ main sentence
Seit(dem) / since *Seit(dem) sie in Wien ist,* Since she has been in Vienna, ↑ temporal clause	*hat er sie nicht gesehen.* he has not seen her. ↑ main sentence

Während / while
Sie spielte Klavier,   *während er Zeitung las.*
She played the piano   while he read the paper.
                ↑   ↑
         main sentence   temporal clause

Other Types of Conjunctions

Obwohl / although
Obwohl er nicht hungrig war,   *aß er sehr viel.*
Although he was not hungry,   he ate a lot.

weil / because
Er bleibt zu Hause,   *weil er krank ist.*
He stays home   because he is sick.

For a further discussion of conjunctions, see Chapter 11.

§3.4 INCOMPLETE SENTENCES

In speaking, we do not always use complete sentences, that is, sentences that have a subject and a predicate. Quite frequently, one or the other part of a sentence is omitted, although it is clearly implied.

Complete Sentence	*Incomplete Sentence*

Wie geht's Ihnen? /
How are you?

Danke, mir geht's gut. /   ↔ *Danke, gut* / Fine,
I'm fine, thank you.   thanks.

Wer spielt hier Klavier? /
Who plays the piano here?

Mein Bruder spielt hier Klavier. /   ↔ *Mein Bruder.* / My
My brother plays the piano here.   brother.

Wo ist deine Schwester? /
Where is your sister?

Meine Schwester ist in der Schule. / ↔ *In der Schule.* / In
My sister is in school.   school.

Parts of Speech

§4.

Nouns

Nouns are words that label or name persons or things (objects, places, concepts, etc.). German nouns sometimes have endings that indicate their gender, number, and role within the sentence, although more often the accompanying article provides this information. All German nouns and words used as nouns are capitalized.

EXAMPLES:

Dieser Mann ist groß. / This man is tall.

↑

> noun (masculine singular)

Diese Frau ist klein. / This woman is small.

↑

> noun (feminine singular)

Diese Rosen sind schön. / These roses are beautiful.

↑

> noun (feminine plural)

There are two main types of nouns:

• Proper nouns name a particular person, place, or thing.

EXAMPLES

Herr Schmidt ist arm. / Mr. Schmidt is poor.

↑

> proper noun

Anton ist glücklich. / Anton is happy.

↑

> proper noun

Spanien ist interessant. / Spain is interesting.
↑

> proper
> noun

- Common nouns do not name a particular person, place, or thing. These can be classified as *count* and *noncount*.
- Count nouns refer to persons, places, or things that can be counted. They have both singular and plural forms.

EXAMPLES:

Singular	Plural
der Tisch / the table	*die Tische* / the tables
die Uhr / the watch	*die Uhren* / the watches
das Kind / the child	*die Kinder* / the children

- Noncount nouns refer to persons, places, or things that cannot be counted; they usually have only a singular form.

EXAMPLES:
der Zucker / the sugar
die Butter / the butter
das Mehl / the flour

§4.2 GENDER

German nouns have three genders: masculine, feminine, and neuter. The gender of a noun is indicated by the definite article that accompanies it: *der* for masculine, *die* for feminine, and *das* for neuter. The grammatical gender does not always coincide with the biological gender. Furthermore, the gender of objects or of abstract nouns can be masculine, feminine, or neuter. Nouns, therefore, should be memorized along with their articles.

§4.2–1 Masculine, Feminine, and Neuter

- Nouns referring to human beings can be masculine, feminine, or neuter.

EXAMPLES:

Masculine	Feminine	Neuter
der Mann / man	*die Frau* / woman	*das Weib* / wife, woman
der Herr / Mr., gentleman	*die Dame* / lady	
der Sohn / son	*die Tochter* / daughter	*das Kind* / child
der Vetter / cousin	*die Kusine* / cousin	*das Mädchen* / girl
der Onkel / uncle	*die Tante* / aunt	*das Fräulein* / young lady, Miss
der Neffe / nephew	*die Nichte* / niece	*das Männlein* / little man

• Nouns ending in -er can also be masculine, feminine, or neuter.

EXAMPLES:

Masculine	Feminine	Neuter
der Vater / father	die Mutter / mother	das Wetter /
der Bruder /	die Schwester /	weather
brother	sister	das Wasser / water
der Teller / plate	die Butter / butter	das Zimmer / room

• Most nouns ending in -el, -ing, or -s are masculine.

EXAMPLES:
der Flügel / wing
der Feigling / coward
der Schlips / tie

• Many nouns ending in -en are also masculine (der Wagen / car), but infinitives used as verbal nouns are always neuter.

EXAMPLES:
das Rauchen / smoking
das Schreiben / writing
das Streben / striving

• Most trees, flowers, and fruit are feminine.

EXAMPLES:
die Tanne / fir tree
die Eiche / oak tree
die Rose / rose
die Nelke / carnation
die Banane / banana
die Birne / pear

> *EXCEPTIONS:*
>
> *der Apfel* / apple
> *der Pfirsich* / peach

• Nouns ending in -age, -ei, -heit, -ie, -ik, -ion, -itis, -keit, -schaft, -tät, -ung, and -ur are feminine.

EXAMPLES:

die Garage / garage	die Pleuritis / pleurisy
die Bäckerei / bakery	die Menschlichkeit / humanity
die Weisheit / wisdom	die Wissenschaft / science
die Melodie / melody	die Universität / university
die Kritik / criticism	die Hoffnung / hope
die Operation / operation	die Natur / nature

- Nouns ending in *-ett, -il, -ium, -ma, -ment, -nis, -tel, -tum,*
  and *-um* (most of them of foreign origin) are neuter.

  EXAMPLES:

  das Ballett / ballet   *das Hindernis* / obstacle
  das Fossil / fossil   *das Zehntel* / tenth
  das Stadium / stage   *das Christentum* / Christianit
  das Klima / climate   *das Album* / album
  das Instrument / instrument

  > EXCEPTIONS:
  >
  > *der Irrtum* / error
  > *der Reichtum* / wealth

- Countries and Cities can be masculine, feminine, or neuter.

  EXAMPLES:

Masculine	Feminine	Neuter
der Iran / Iran	*die Türkei* / Turkey	*das Spanien* /
der Libanon /	*die Schweiz* /	Spain
Lebanon	Switzerland	*das Wien* / Vienna
der Sudan / Sudan	*die Normandie* /	*das Rom* / Rome
	Normandy	

- Some masculine nouns referring to male persons have
  corresponding feminine nouns ending in *-in* that refer to
  female persons.

  EXAMPLES:

Masculine	Feminine
der Arbeiter / male worker	*die Arbeiterin* / female worke
der Sänger / male singer	*die Sängerin* / female singer
der Arzt / male physician	*die Ärztin* / female physician
der Student / male student	*die Studentin* / female studer
der König / king	*die Königin* / queen
der Graf / count	*die Gräfin* / countess

- Diminutives ending in *-chen* or *-lein* are neuter.

  These endings convey smallness or affection.

  EXAMPLES:

Noun	Corresponding Diminutive
Paul	*Paulchen* / little Paul
Grete	*Gretchen* / little Grete
der Stern / star	*das Sternchen* / little star
die Maus / mouse	*das Mäuschen* / little mouse
das Bild / picture	*das Bildchen* / little picture
der Mann	*das Männlein* / little man
die Rose	*das Röslein* / little rose

§4.2–2
Nouns Having More than One Gender

There is a group of German nouns whose meaning depends on gender (determined by the definitite article—see Chapter 5). For example:

Der Erbe is your male heir, who will inherit what you own. (Feminine and plural forms also exist: *die Erbin* / heiress; *Erben* / heirs). *Das Erbe* is the inheritance that he will inherit.

OTHER EXAMPLES:

Masculine	Feminine or Neuter
der Band / volume	*das Band* / ribbon
der Flur / corridor	*die Flur* / field
der Gehalt / contents	*das Gehalt* / salary
der Junge / boy	*das Junge* / offspring of an animal
der Kunde / customer	*die Kunde* / news
der Leiter / manager	*die Leiter* / ladder
der Schild / shield	*das Schild* / sign
der See / lake	*die See* / sea, ocean
der Tor / fool	*das Tor* / gate
der Verdienst / earnings	*das Verdienst* / merit

§4.2–3
Compound Nouns

By combining two or more nouns, compound nouns are formed. The last noun of the compound noun determines the gender. Two singular nouns may be joined to form a compound noun, or a singular noun and a plural noun may be joined.

Noun 1	Noun 2	Noun 3	Compound Noun
der Winter / winter	*der Mantel* / coat		*der Wintermantel* / winter coat
der Zahn / tooth	*die Bürste* / brush		*die Zahnbürste* / toothbrush
der Motor / motor	*das Boot* / boat		*das Motorboot* / motor boat
die Karten / cards	*das Spiel* / game		*das Kartenspiel* / card game
die Straßen / streets	*die Bahn* / railroad		*die Straßenbahn* / street car
der Raum / space	*das Schiff* / ship	*die Fahrt* / ride	*die Raumschiffahrt* / space travel
die Augen / eyes	*die Zeugen* / witnesses	*der Bericht* / report	*der Augenzeugenbericht* / eyewitness report

Sometimes, compound nouns are joined together by the letter *s*.

Noun 1	Noun 2	Noun 3	Compound Noun
das Volk / people	*der Wagen* / car		*der Volkswagen* / people's car (VW)
der Frühling / spring	*das Fest* / festival		*das Frühlingsfest* / spring festival
die Geburt / birth	*der Tag* / day	*die Feier* / celebration	*die Geburtstagsfeier* / birthday celebration

§4.3
NUMBER

Number means that a word can be *singular* (referring to one person, thing, etc.) or *plural* (referring to more than one).

- We have briefly discussed the difference between count and noncount nouns. Here are some more noncount nouns that can be used in the singular only.

    EXAMPLES:
    das Wasser / water
    die Milch / milk
    das Salz / salt
    der Hunger / hunger
    der Durst / thirst
    der Reichtum / wealth
    die Gesundheit / health

- Some nouns are singular in German but plural in English.

    EXAMPLES:
    die Brille / eyeglasses
    die Hose / pants
    die Schere / scissors

- Other nouns are plural in German but singular in English.

    EXAMPLES:
    die Flitterwochen / honeymoon
    die Möbel / furniture
    die Ferien / vacation

- There are no definite rules for the formation of noun plurals. The plural is recognized by the article or by the context. The noun plural should be memorized along with the singular. The plural article for all three genders is *die.* You will find more about the formation of plurals on the following pages.

§4.4
DECLENSION
OF NOUNS

Declension relates to the endings of a noun that determine its role within a sentence. *Case* is the inflectional form of a noun indicating its grammatical relation to other words.

- The German noun has four cases: The *nominative,* marking the subject of a verb; the *accusative,* or the direct object; the *dative,* or the indirect object; the *genitive,* or the possessive.

EXAMPLE:

Der Hund The dog	bringt brings	der Mutter to the mother	das Buch the book	des Mädchens. of the girl.
subject ↕ nominative ↕ who?	verb	indirect object ↕ dative ↕ to whom?	direct object ↕ accusative ↕ what?	possessive ↕ genitive ↕ whose?

§4.4 – 1
Singular

Masculine nouns with the endings -s or -es in the genitive are called masculine 1 (strong). Those ending in -en in the accusative, dative, and genitive are called masculine 2 (weak).

Case	Masculine 1	Meaning	Masculine 2	Meaning
nom.	der Vater	the father (subj.)	der Junge	the boy (subj.)
acc.	den Vater	the father (obj.)	den Jungen	the boy (obj.)
dat.	dem Vater	to the father	dem Jungen	to the boy
gen.	des Vaters	of the father	des Jungen	of the boy

Neuter nouns have a genitive ending of -s or -es only.

Case	Noun	Meaning	Noun	Meaning
nom.	das Buch	the book (subj.)	das Geschäft	the business (subj.)
acc.	das Buch	the book (obj.)	das Geschäft	the business (obj.)
dat.	dem Buch	to the book	dem Geschäft	to the business
gen.	des Buches	of the book	des Geschäfts	of the business

Feminine nouns take *no* endings:

Case	Noun	Meaning	Noun	Meaning
nom.	die Katze	the cat (subj.)	die Frau	the woman (subj.)
acc.	die Katze	the cat (obj.)	die Frau	the woman (obj.)
dat.	der Katze	to the cat	der Frau	to the woman
gen.	der Katze	of the cat	der Frau	of the woman

Whether to use the -s or the -es as a genitive ending depends on the structure of the noun.

- For reasons of pronounciation, all nouns ending in sibilants (such as -s, -ß, -sch, -z, or -zt) take the -es ending.

Case	Noun	Meaning
nom.	das Gas	the gas
gen.	des Gases	of the gas
nom.	der Ruß	the soot
gen.	des Rußes	of the soot
nom.	der Fisch	the fish
gen.	des Fisches	of the fish
nom.	der Arzt	the physician
gen.	des Arztes	of the physician

- The ending -es is preferred for nouns of one syllable, nouns with a stressed last syllable, or nouns ending with two or more consonants.

Case	Noun	Meaning
nom.	der Tag	the day
gen.	des Tages	of the day
nom.	der Vertrag	the contract
gen.	des Vertrages	of the contract
nom.	der Kampf	the fight
gen.	des Kampfes	of the fight

- The shorter ending -s must be used if the noun ends in -en, -em. -el, or -er.

Case	Noun	Meaning
nom.	der Wagen	the car
gen.	des Wagens	of the car
nom.	der Atem	the breath
gen.	des Atems	of the breath
nom.	der Kessel	the kettle
gen.	des Kessels	of the kettle
nom.	der Führer	the leader
gen.	des Führers	of the leader

- The ending -s is preferred for nouns that end with an unstressed syllable.

Case	Noun	Meaning
nom.	*der Urlaub*	the vacation
gen.	*des Urlaubs*	of the vacation
nom.	*der Vortrag*	the lecture
gen.	*des Vortrags*	of the lecture
nom.	*der Abend*	the evening
gen.	*des Abends*	of the evening
nom.	*der Jüngling*	the young man
gen.	*des Jünglings*	of the young man

- The dative singular in masculine and neuter nouns of one syllable can take the optional ending of -e.

Case	Noun	Meaning
dat.	*dem Hund(e)*	to the dog
dat.	*dem Buch(e)*	to the book

§4.4 – 2
Plural

How do German plurals compare with their English counterparts? Almost all English nouns form plurals by adding -s or -es to the singular forms: girl, girls; house, houses. In German, there is a relatively small number of nouns that add -s to form the plural. Many nouns add various other endings, with or without an umlaut. Some plural forms do not change at all from the singular. As pointed out before, the only safe way is to learn the plural along with the genitive singular of the noun. If in doubt, consult a dictionary. In terms of forming plurals, most German nouns belong to one of five groups. Each group forms the plural endings in a different way.

Group 1

Nouns in Group 1 do not change in the plural, except for adding -n in the dative (unless the -n is there already). Some plural forms take the umlaut. Most of these nouns take the endings -chen, -lein, -el, -en or -er. They are mostly neuter or masculine.

Case	Singular	Plural	Meaning
nom.	*der Bruder*	*die Brüder*	the brother(s) (subj.)
acc.	*den Bruder*	*die Brüder*	the brother(s) (obj.)
dat.	*dem Bruder*	*den Brüdern*	to the brother(s)
gen.	*des Bruders*	*der Brüder*	of the brother(s)
nom.	*die Mutter*	*die Mütter*	the mother(s) (subj.)
acc.	*die Mutter*	*die Mütter*	the mother(s) (obj.)
dat.	*der Mutter*	*den Müttern*	to the mother(s)
gen.	*der Mutter*	*der Mütter*	of the mother(s)
nom.	*das Mädchen*	*die Mädchen*	the girl(s) (subj.)
acc.	*das Mädchen*	*die Mädchen*	the girl(s) (obj.)
dat.	*dem Mädchen*	*den Mädchen*	to the girl(s)
gen.	*des Mädchens*	*der Mädchen*	of the girl(s)

EXAMPLES:

der Apfel / apple (accusative singular)
Ich esse den Apfel. / I eat the apple.

das Fräulein / young lady (dative singular)
Ich danke dem Fräulein. / I thank the young lady.

der Mantel / coat (nominative plural)
Wo sind unsere Mäntel? / Where are our coats?

der Lehrer / teacher (dative plural)
Er spricht mit den Lehrern. / He talks with the teachers.

Group 2

Nouns belonging to Group 2 add -*e* (-*en* in the dative) to form plurals. Plural vowels sometimes take the umlaut. Most of these nouns — which may be masculine, feminine, or neuter — consist of one syllable.

Case	Singular	Plural	Meaning
nom.	*der Brief*	*die Briefe*	the letter(s) (subj.)
acc.	*den Brief*	*die Briefe*	the letter(s) (obj.)
dat.	*dem Brief*	*den Briefen*	to the letter(s)
gen.	*des Briefes*	*der Briefe*	of the letter(s)

Case	Singular	Plural	Meaning
nom.	die Hand	die Hände	the hand(s) (subj.)
acc.	die Hand	die Hände	the hand(s) (obj.)
dat.	der Hand	den Händen	to the hand(s)
gen.	der Hand	der Hände	of the hand(s)
nom.	das Tier	die Tiere	the animal(s) (subj.)
acc.	das Tier	die Tiere	the animal(s) (obj.)
dat.	dem Tier	den Tieren	to the animal(s)
gen.	des Tieres	der Tiere	of the animal(s)

EXAMPLES:

der Tisch / table (genitive singular)
Er sitzt am Ende des Tisches. / He sits at the end of
  the table.

die Stadt / city (accusative singular)
Er besucht die Stadt. / He visits the city.

der Hund / dog (dative plural)
Gib den Hunden Wasser! / Give water to the dogs.

die Wurst / sausage (accusative plural)
Heute essen wir die Würste. / Today we'll eat the
  sausages.

Group 3

Nouns in Group 3 add -er (-ern in the dative) to form the
plural. As in Group 2, plural vowels (or diphthongs) sometimes take the umlaut. There are no feminine nouns in this
declension.

Case	Singular	Plural	Meaning
nom.	der Mann	die Männer	the man (men) (subj.)
acc.	den Mann	die Männer	the man (men) (obj.)
dat.	dem Mann	den Männern	to the man (men)
gen.	des Mannes	der Männer	of the man (men)
nom.	das Bild	die Bilder	the picture(s) (subj.)
acc.	das Bild	die Bilder	the picture(s) (obj.)
dat.	dem Bild	den Bildern	to the picture(s)
gen.	des Bildes	der Bilder	of the picture(s)

Case	Singular	Plural	Meaning
nom.	*das Haus*	*die Häuser*	the house(s) (subj.)
acc.	*das Haus*	*die Häuser*	the house(s) (obj.)
dat.	*dem Haus*	*den Häusern*	to the house(s)
gen.	*des Hauses*	*der Häuser*	of the house(s)

EXAMPLES:

Das Buch / book (accusative singular)
Er liest das Buch. / He is reading the book.

das Kind / child (genitive singular)
Das ist der Ball des Kindes. / That is the child's ball.

der Wurm / worm (nominative plural)
Die Würmer sind in der Erde. / The worms are in the soil.

Gott / god (dative plural)
Sie beten zu den Göttern. / They pray to the gods.

Note: Nouns in Groups 1, 2, and 3 have the "strong" declension, in which the singular genitive takes an *-s* or *-es*. Some of the nouns take the umlaut. If in doubt about its proper use, please consult a dictionary.

Group 4

Nouns in Group 4 add *-n* or *-en* to the singular to form all four cases of the plural; they never take the umlaut. Most of these nouns are feminine. There are no neuter nouns in this group.

Case	Singular	Plural	Meaning
nom.	*die Schule*	*die Schulen*	the school(s) (subj.)
acc.	*die Schule*	*die Schulen*	the school(s) (obj.)
dat.	*der Schule*	*den Schulen*	to the school(s)
gen.	*der Schule*	*der Schulen*	of the school(s)
nom.	*die Antwort*	*die Antworten*	the answer(s) (subj.)
acc.	*die Antwort*	*die Antworten*	the answer(s) (obj.)
dat.	*der Antwort*	*den Antworten*	to the answer(s)
gen.	*der Antwort*	*der Antworten*	of the answer(s)

Case	Singular	Plural	Meaning
nom.	die Studentin	die Studentinnen	the female student(s) (subj.)
acc.	die Studentin	die Studentinnen	the female student(s) (obj.)
dat.	der Studentin	den Studentinnen	to the female student(s)
gen.	der Studentin	der Studentinnen	of the female student(s)
nom.	der Mensch	die Menschen	the human being(s) (subj.)
acc.	den Menschen	die Menschen	the human being(s) (obj.)
dat.	dem Menschen	den Menschen	to the human being(s)
gen.	des Menschen	der Menschen	of the human being(s)

- Nouns ending with -in add -nen in the plural:

    die Doktorin / woman doctor
    die Doktorinnen / women doctors

- Most masculine nouns in this group denote living beings:

    der Junge / boy
    der Elefant / elephant

- This group has also been called the "weak" declension because of its -en endings. Masculine singular nouns add -en to form the accusative, dative, and genitive.

    EXAMPLES:

der Held / hero (accusative singular)   Amerika ehrte den Helden. / America honored the hero.
die Tante / aunt (dative singular)   Sie schuldet der Tante Geld. / She owes money to the aunt.
die Schwester / sister (nominative plural)   Die Schwestern spielen im Garten. / The sisters play in the garden.
der Bär / bear (dative plural)   Er fütterte einen von den Bären. / He fed one of the bears.

Group 5

Most nouns in Group 5 are of foreign origin. Their declension is similar to that of English nouns. They add the ending -s to the singular to form the plural.

There is no -n ending in the dative plural. Nouns in this group can be masculine, feminine, or neuter.

Case	Singular	Plural	Meaning
nom.	*der Park*	*die Parks*	the park(s) (subj.)
acc.	*den Park*	*die Parks*	the park(s) (obj.)
dat.	*dem Park*	*den Parks*	to the park(s)
gen.	*des Parks*	*der Parks*	of the park(s)
nom.	*die Kamera*	*die Kameras*	the camera(s) (subj.)
acc.	*die Kamera*	*die Kameras*	the camera(s) (obj.)
dat.	*der Kamera*	*den Kameras*	to the camera(s)
gen.	*der Kamera*	*der Kameras*	of the camera(s)
nom.	*das Radio*	*die Radios*	the radio(s) (subj.)
acc.	*das Radio*	*die Radios*	the radio(s) (obj.)
dat.	*dem Radio*	*den Radios*	to the radio(s)
gen.	*des Radios*	*der Radios*	of the radio(s)

EXAMPLES:

der Streik | strike (genitive singular)
Wegen des Streiks sind die Läden zu. | Because of the strike, the stores are closed.

die Bar | bar (accusative singular)
Kennst du diese Bar? | Do you know this bar?

das Kino | the movie theater (accusative plural)
Ich kenne alle Kinos in der Stadt. | I know all the movie theaters in the city.

das Restaurant / restaurant (dative plural)
In diesen Restaurants ißt man gut. / One eats well in these restaurants.

The following table summarizes the plural endings of nouns in Groups 1 through 5.

Group	Singular	Plural	Explanation
1	*der Löffel* / spoon *das Zimmer* / room	*die Löffel* / spoons *die Zimmer* / rooms	No plural endings
	der Vater / father *die Tochter* / daughter *das Kloster* / convent	*die Väter* / fathers *die Töchter* / daughters *die Klöster* / convents	Plurals take the umlaut.

Group	Singular	Plural	Explanation
2	der Hund / dog das Schaf / sheep	die Hunde / dogs die Schafe / sheep	Plurals end in -e; no umlauts.
	der Zug / train die Nacht / night das Floß / raft	die Züge / trains die Nächte / nights die Flöße / rafts	Plurals end in -e and take the umlaut.
3	der Leib / body das Ei / egg	die Leiber / bodies die Eier / eggs	Plurals end in -er; no umlauts.
	der Gott / god das Glas / glass	die Götter / gods die Gläser / glasses	Plurals end in -er and take the umlaut.
4	der Junge / boy die Antwort / answer das Bett / bed	die Jungen / boys die Antworten / answers die Betten / beds	Plurals end in -(e)n; no umlauts.
5	der Job / job die Bar / bar das Echo / echo	die Jobs / jobs die Bars / bars die Echos / echos	Plurals end in -s; no umlauts.

§4.4–3
Irregular
Nouns

There are some irregular nouns that, according to their plural endings (-en), should belong to Group 4. They are irregular because, instead of adding -s, -es, or -en to form the genitive singular, they add -ns or -ens.

Case	Singular	Plural	Meaning
nom.	das Herz	die Herzen	the heart(s) (subj.)
acc.	das Herz	die Herzen	the heart(s) (obj.)
dat.	dem Herzen	den Herzen	to the heart(s)
gen.	des Herzens	der Herzen	of the heart(s)
nom.	der Name	die Namen	the name(s) (subj.)
acc.	den Namen	die Namen	the name(s) (obj.)
dat.	dem Namen	den Namen	to the name(s)
gen.	des Namens	der Namen	of the name(s)

EXAMPLES:

> der Glaube / faith (accusative singular)
> Er behielt seinen Glauben. / He kept his faith.

> der Wille / will (genitive singular)
> Es war ein Akt des Willens. / It was an act of will.

> der Gedanke / thought (nominative plural)
> Die Gedanken sind frei. / Thoughts are free.

§4.4–4
Nouns with Mixed Declensions

The declension of these nouns is strong in the singular (the singular genitive ends in -s or -es), and it is weak in the plural (each plural ending is -en). There are no feminine nouns in this declension. Mixed-declension nouns do not take an umlaut.

Case	Singular	Plural	Meaning
nom.	der Schmerz	die Schmerzen	the pain(s) (subj.)
acc.	den Schmerz	die Schmerzen	the pain(s) (obj.)
dat.	dem Schmerz	den Schmerzen	to the pain(s)
gen.	des Schmerzes	der Schmerzen	of the pain(s)
nom.	das Auge	die Augen	the eye(s) (subj.)
acc.	das Auge	die Augen	the eye(s) (obj.)
dat.	dem Auge	den Augen	to the eye(s)
gen.	des Auges	der Augen	of the eye(s)

- Also belonging to the mixed declension are many foreign words, derived from Latin or Greek, with the endings -ma or -um in the singular and -en in the plural.

Case	Singular	Plural	Meaning
nom.	das Thema	die Themen	the theme(s) (subj.)
acc.	das Thema	die Themen	the theme(s) (obj.)
dat.	dem Thema	den Themen	to the theme(s)
gen.	des Themas	der Themen	of the theme(s)
nom.	das Datum	die Daten	the date(s) (subj.)
acc.	das Datum	die Daten	the date(s) (obj.)
dat.	dem Datum	den Daten	to the date(s)
gen.	des Datums	der Daten	of the date(s)
nom.	das Museum	die Museen	the museum(s) (subj.)
acc.	das Museum	die Museen	the museum(s) (obj.)
dat.	dem Museum	den Museen	to the museum(s)
gen.	des Museums	der Museen	of the museum(s)

- Some foreign words ending in -us keep their ending in all four cases of the singular, but take the ending -en in the plural.

Case	Singular	Plural	Meaning
nom.	der Organismus	die Organismen	the organism(s) (subj.)
acc.	den Organismus	die Organismen	the organism(s) (obj.)
dat.	dem Organismus	den Organismen	to the organism(s)
gen.	des Organismus	der Organismen	of the organism(s)

Case	Singular	Plural	Meaning
nom.	der Rhythmus	die Rhythmen	the rhythm(s) (subj.)
acc.	den Rhythmus	die Rhythmen	the rhythm(s) (obj.)
dat.	dem Rhythmus	den Rhythmen	to the rhythm(s)
gen.	des Rhythmus	der Rhythmen	of the rhythm(s)

EXAMPLES:

> das Drama / drama (genitive singular)
> Ich kenne den Inhalt des Dramas. / I know the meaning
> of the drama.

> der Realismus / realism (accusative singular)
> Ich bewundere den Realismus dieses Romans. / I
> admire the realism of this novel.

> das Museum / museum (genitive plural)
> Der Reichtum dieser Museen ist erstaunlich. / The
> wealth of these museums is amazing.

§4.5
THE SAXON
GENITIVE

The Saxon genitive is an abbreviated form of the regular
genitive; it can be used with proper names that have no
endings in the accusative and dative.

- The Saxon genitive is used by adding an -s to the proper
name:

  Pauls Haus / Paul's house

- It can either precede the subject or follow it. In the latter
case, the subject takes an article.

  EXAMPLES
  Michaels Vater / Michael's father
  Evas Garten / Eve's garden
  OR
  Der Vater Michaels / the father of Michael
  Der Garten Evas / the garden of Eve.

  Note that in German there is no apostrophe preceding
  the Saxon genitive ending -s.

- Proper names preceded by the genitive articles des or der
do not add the -s.

  EXAMPLES:
  Der Vater des Michael / the father of Michael
  Der Garten der Eva / the garden of Eve

- Words indicating family relationships (except *Bruder* and *Schwester*) also can be used in the Saxon genitive.

  EXAMPLES:
  Onkels Schuhe / uncle's shoes
  Mutters Kleid / mother's dress

- Place names follow the same rules as proper names.

  EXAMPLES:
  Belgiens Hauptstadt / Belgium's capital
  Roms Ruinen / Rome's ruins
                            OR
  die Hauptstadt Belgiens / The capital of Belgium
  die Ruinen Roms / The ruins of Rome

- The preposition *von* (of) is usually used instead of the Saxon genitive if the proper names end in *-s, -ß, -x,* or *-z.*

  EXAMPLES:
  die Bauten von Adolf Loos / the buildings of Adolf Loos
  die Opern von Richard Strauß / the operas of Richard Strauß
  der Anzug von Max / the suit of Max (Max's suit)
  die Krawatte von Franz / the tie of Franz (Franz's tie)

- The preposition *von* plus the dative is sometimes used instead of the genitive to avoid stilted phrases.

  EXAMPLES:
  die Gesundheit von vielen anderen / the health of many others
  Er ist ein Freund von dem (vom) Bruder des Direktors. / He is a friend of the brother of the director (of the director's brother)

When studying German nouns, it is strongly recommended that you memorize them along with their gender (*m.* for masculine, *f.* for feminine, *n.* for neuter), the genitive singular, and the nominative plural.

Dictionary Word	Gender	Genitive Singular	Nominative Plural	Meaning
Apfel	*m.*	-s	¨	Apfels, Äpfel
Stunde	*f.*	—	-n	Stunde, Stunden
Bild	*n.*	-es	-er	Bildes, Bilder

Most dictionaries will also give pronunciation, stress, and part of speech.

Articles

Articles are words placed before nouns (or their modifying adjectives) that permit us to differentiate among them in some way.

- Articles that refer to specific persons or objects are called *definite articles* (equivalent to the English "the"). Articles designating nonspecific persons or objects are called *indefinite articles* (equivalent to the English "a" or "an").

Definite	Indefinite
der Tisch / **the** table	*ein Tisch* / **a** table
der braune Tisch / **the** brown table	*ein brauner Tisch* / **a** brown table

- In German the article, when used in the singular, indicates the grammatical gender of the noun (masculine, feminine, or neuter).

  der Zug / the train
  die Blume / the flower
  das Papier / the paper

- All articles agree with the nouns that follow in gender and number.

  der Mann / the man
  die Männer / the men

  Demonstratives will also be included in this chapter because there are striking similarities between them and the definite article.

The *definite article* points to people, objects, or concepts that are known or have been defined.

FORMS OF THE DEFINITE ARTICLE				
	Singular			**Plural**	
Case	**Masculine**	**Feminine**	**Neuter**	**All Genders**	**Meaning**
nom.	der	die	das	die	the
acc.	den	die	das	die	the
dat.	dem	der	dem	den	to the
gen	des	der	des	der	of the

Here are some examples of how the different forms of the definite article are used in sentences:

Masculine Singular
Der *Baum ist groß.* / The tree is big. *Sie pflanzte* ***den*** *Baum.* / She planted the tree. *Sie gab* ***dem*** *Baum Wasser.* / She gave the tree water. *Sie sitzt im Schatten* ***des*** *Baums.* / She sits in the shade of the tree.

Feminine Singular
Die *Rose ist schön.* / The rose is beautiful. *Er pflückt* ***die*** *Rose.* / He picks the rose. *Er gibt sie* ***der*** *Frau.* / He gives it to the woman. *Sie riecht den Duft* ***der*** *Rose.* / She smells the fragrance of the rose.

Neuter Singular
Das *Mädchen arbeitet hier.* / The girl works here. *Er liebt* ***das*** *Mädchen.* / He loves the girl. *Er schreibt* ***dem*** *Mädchen.* / He writes to the girl. *Er hat den Ring* ***des*** *Mädchens.* / He has the girl's ring.

Plural
Die *Kinder kommen.* / The children are coming. *Oma liebt* ***die*** *Kinder.* / Grandma loves the children. *Sie hilft* ***den*** *Kindern.* / She helps the children. *Sie sucht die Spielzeuge* ***der*** *Kinder.* / She looks for the children's toys.

In German the definite article is used more often than in English.

- It is used with many abstract nouns.

  EXAMPLES:
  Die Natur ist schön. / Nature is beautiful.
  Das Schicksal ist grausam. / Fate is cruel.
  Der Tod ist tragisch. / Death is tragic.

- It is used whenever the noun has a collective or generalized meaning.

  EXAMPLES:
  Der Mensch ist sterblich. / Man is mortal.
  Die Liebe ist eine Himmelsmacht. / Love is a heavenly power.

- It is used when expressing familiarity with works of litera-
  ture, music, or fictional characters.

  EXAMPLES:
  Ich habe den Hamlet ganz vergessen. / I totally forgot *Hamlet.*
  Sie hat gestern die Aida gesungen. / She sang Aida yesterday.

- It is used with proper names that are identified by an adjective.

  EXAMPLES:
  der kleine Paul / little Paul
  der dumme Hans / stupid Hans

- It is also used with certain geographical terms.

  EXAMPLES:
  Die Friedrichstraße ist in Berlin. / Friedrich Street is in Berlin.
  Der Baikalsee ist in Sibirien. / Lake Baikal is in Siberia.

- The definite article is used when expressing a date.

  EXAMPLES:
  Morgen ist der 10. März. / Tomorrow is March 10.
  Frankfurt, den 4. Oktober 1986. / Frankfurt, October 4, 1986.

- It is also used with weights and measures.

  EXAMPLES:
  Das kostet 20 Mark das Kilo. / That costs 20 marks per kilo.
  Das ist 50 Mark den Meter. / That is 50 marks per meter.

5.3
THE
INDEFINITE
ARTICLE

The *indefinite article* points to something that is unspecified
— a person or an object in the singular. There are no plural
forms.

FORMS OF THE INDEFINITE ARTICLE				
Case	Masculine	Feminine	Neuter	Meaning
nom.	ein	eine	ein	a, an
acc.	einen	eine	ein	a, an
dat.	einem	einer	einem	to a, to an
gen.	eines	einer	eines	of a, of an

The use of the indefinite article in German is quite similar to its use in English. Here are some examples:

Masculine
Ein Junge spielt dort. / A boy plays there. *Er hat einen Wagen.* / He has a car. *Ich schreibe einem Freund.* / I'm writing a friend. *Das ist der Hut eines Mannes.* / That is a man's hat.

Feminine
Eine Frau ist here. / A woman is here. *Er nimmt eine Pille.* / He takes a pill. *Sie hilft einer Freundin.* / She helps a girl friend. *Das ist der Name einer Firma.* / That is the name of a firm.

Neuter
Ein Hotel ist um die Ecke. / A hotel is around the corner. *Karl gibt mir ein Glas.* / Karl gives me a glass. *Er schreibt einem Kind.* / He writes to a child. *Das sind die Schuhe eines Mädchens.* / Those are a girl's shoes.

- The indefinite article is omitted after the verbs *sein* (to be) and *werden* (to become).

  EXAMPLES:
  Ich bin Deutscher. / I am a German.
  Mein Vater ist Ingenieur. / My father is an engineer.
  Er wird Arzt. / He becomes a physician.

- It is omitted after the conjunction *als* (meaning "as").

  EXAMPLES:
  Als Kind tat ich das oft. / I often did that as a child.
  Ich war in Ägypten als Arzt. / I was in Egypt as a doctor.

- It is also omitted in certain phrases referring to the body.

  EXAMPLES:
  Er hat Bauchweh. / He has a stomach ache.
  Sie hat Zahnschmerzen. / She has a toothache.
  Sie hat Temperatur. / She has a temperature.

§5.4 DEMONSTRATIVES

Demonstratives point to a person or thing that has been referred to previously. They specify whether someone or something is relatively near (the demonstratives "this," and "these") or far ("that" and "those").

DEMONSTRATIVES INDICATING "NEARNESS"

Case	Masculine	Feminine	Neuter	Meaning
Singular				
nom.	der, dieser	die, diese	das, dieses	this one, this
acc.	den, diesen	die, diese	das, dieses	this one, this
dat.	dem, diesem	der, dieser	dem, diesem	to this one, to this
gen.	dessen, dieses	deren, dieser	dessen, dieses	of this
Plural				
nom.	die, diese	Same as masculine.		these
acc.	die, diese			these
dat.	den, denen, diesen			to these
gen.	deren, derer, dieser			of these

The genitive forms of the demonstrative *der* (*dessen, deren,* and *derer*) are rarely used.

- *Der, die,* and *das* are the most frequently used demonstratives. Standing by themselves, they function as demonstrative pronouns and are translated as "this one" or "that one." In addition, they also serve as more emphatic personal pronouns than *er* / *sie* (he / she).

  Der ist sehr nett. / This one (He) is very nice.
  Die ist sehr schön. / That one (She) is very beautiful.

- Preceding the noun, they function as demonstrative adjectives, and can be used interchangeably with *dieser:*

  Der (dieser) Mann ist sehr nett. / This man is very nice.

- When spoken, they take a strong stress. They differ from the definite article in all genitive forms (rarely used) and in the dative plural.

Demonstratives Used as Pronouns

Den muß ich sehen. / **That one** (Him) I must see.
Dem glaube ich nicht. / I do not believe **him**.
Die kenne ich. / I know **them**.

Demonstratives Used as Adjectives

Diese (die) Frau ist schön. / **This** woman is beautiful.
Dieser (der) Junge ist mein Bruder. / **This** boy is my brother.
Diesen (den) Studenten kenne ich. / I know **this** student.

- The neuter form of *dieser* may be shortened to *dies:*

  Dies ist ein schönes Kleid. / This is a beautiful dress.
  Dies Buch ist sehr gut. / This book is very good.

		DEMONSTRATIVES INDICATING "FARTHER AWAY"			
	Case	**Masculine**	**Feminine**	**Neuter**	**Meaning**
S i n g u l a r	nom.	jener	jene	jenes	that one, that
	acc.	jenen	jene	jenes	that one, that
	dat.	jenem	jener	jenem	to that one, to that
	gen.	jenes	jener	jenes	of that one, of that
P l u r a l	nom.	jene	Same as masculine.		those
	acc.	jene			those
	dat.	jenen			to those
	gen.	jener			of those

EXAMPLES:

jener Mann / that man   *jenen Leuten* / to those people
jenes Kind / that child   *jener Mädchen* / of those girls
jene Frau / that woman   *jene Personen* / those persons

- *Dieser,* used as a demonstrative adjective (preceding a noun), corresponds in usage to both "this" and "that."

  an diesem Tag / on this day OR on that day

- However, the meaning of *dieser* is restricted to "this" if it i contrasted to *jener* "that."

  Dieser Wein schmeckt besser als jener. / This wine tastes better than that one.

- Where there is no such contrast, *jener* expresses more remoteness than the English "that." It is cognate to the English "yonder" and is not used very frequently. More colloquially, *da* (there) and *da drüben* (over there) are use to express remoteness from the speaker.

  Siehst du den Baum da? / Do you see the tree there?

§6.

Adjectives

Adjectives are words that describe or modify nouns. An adjective must agree with the noun that it modifies in gender and number.

> *das hübsche Kind* / the pretty child
> *der nette Junge* / the nice boy
> *die schönen Kleider* / the beautiful clothes

§6.1 DECLENSION OF ADJECTIVES

§6.1–1 Weak Endings

If the adjective is preceded by words like *der* (the), *dieser* (this), *jener* (that), *jeder* (each), *welcher* (which), *solcher* (such), or *all(er)* (all), it takes the following "weak" endings:

| Case | Singular | | | Plural |
	Masculine	Feminine	Neuter	All Genders
nom.	-e	-e	-e	-en
acc.	-en	-e	-e	-en
dat.	-en	-en	-en	-en
gen.	-en	-en	-en	-en

Case	Masculine Singular	Feminine Singular
nom.	*der neue Hut* / the new hat	*die gute Frau* / the good woman
acc.	*den neuen Hut* / the new hat	*die gute Frau* / the good woman
dat.	*dem neuen Hut* / to the new hat	*der guten Frau* / to the good woman
gen.	*des neuen Hutes* / of the new hat	*der guten Frau* / of the good woman

57

Case	Neuter Singular	Plural
nom.	*das alte Radio* / the old radio	*die neuen Hüte* / the new hat
acc.	*das alte Radio* / the old radio	*die neuen Hüte* / the new hat
dat.	*dem alten Radio* / to the old radio	*den neuen Hüten* / to the new hats
gen.	*des alten Radios* / of the old radio	*der neuen Hüte* / of the new hats

EXAMPLES:
Ich mag den neuen Anzug. / I like the new suit.
Er dankt der guten Mutter. / He thanks the good mother.
Sie haßt die kalten Winter. / She hates the cold winters.
Ich bewundere das Talent dieses großen Dichters. / I admire the talent of this great poet.
Ich gehe spazieren an jedem schönen Tag. / I take a walk on each nice day.
Wir haben nur den alten Katalog. / We have only the old catalogue.
Welcher alte Mann sagte das? / Which old man said that?

§6.1–2 Strong Endings

If the adjective is *not* preceded by any of the words mentioned above, it takes "strong" endings.

Case	Singular			Plural
	Masculine	**Feminine**	**Neuter**	**All Gender**
nom.	*-er*	*-e*	*-es*	*-e*
acc.	*-en*	*-e*	*-es*	*-e*
dat.	*-em*	*-er*	*-em*	*-en*
gen.	*-en*	*-er*	*-en*	*-er*

Case	Masculine Singular	Feminine Singular
nom.	*alter Baum* / old tree	*frische Erde* / fresh soil
acc.	*alten Baum* / old tree	*frische Erde* / fresh soil
dat.	*altem Baum* / to an old tree	*frischer Erde* / to fresh so
gen.	*alten Baumes* / of an old tree	*frischer Erde* / of fresh sc

Case	Neuter Singular	Plural
nom.	*junges Mädchen* / young girl	*alte Bäume* / old trees
acc.	*junges Mädchen* / young girl	*frische Rosen* / fresh roses
dat.	*jungem Mädchen* / to a young girl	*jungen Mädchen* / to young girls
gen.	*jungen Mädchens* / of a young girl	*neuer Bücher* / of new books

EXAMPLES:

Netter Junge, dein Sohn! / Nice boy, your son.
Schlechten Wetters wegen bleibt er zu Hause. / Because of the bad weather, he stays at home.
Er ist in großer Eile. / He is in a big hurry.
Sie ist guten Mutes. / She is of good cheer.
Ich liebe alte Sachen. / I love old things.

• Adjectives preceded by indefinite pronouns or numerals take strong endings:

andere gute Freunde / other good friends
verschiedene schöne Bücher / various beautiful books
viele neue Kleider / many new clothes
wenige alte Sachen / few old things
zehn kleine Kinder / ten little children
but: die zehn kleinen Kinder / the ten little children

EXCEPTION: when using *keine* and *alle,* the adjective following these indefinite expressions takes the weak endings:

keine neuen Kleider / no new clothes
alle guten Freunde / all good friends

§6.1–3
Mixed Endings

If the adjective is preceded by words like *ein* (a, one), its negative *kein* (no, none), or the possessive adjectives (see §6.3) *mein* (my, mine), *dein*, *Ihr* (your), *sein* (his), *ihr* (her), *unser* (our), *euer* (your), or *ihr* (their), it takes the following endings:

Case	Singular			Plural
	Masculine	**Feminine**	**Neuter**	**All Genders**
nom.	-er	-e	-es	-en
acc.	-en	-e	-es	-en
dat.	-en	-en	-en	-en
gen.	-en	-en	-en	-en

Case	Masculine Singular	Feminine Singular
nom.	*ein neuer Hut* / a new hat	*eine gute Frau* / a good woman
acc.	*einen neuen Hut* / a new hat	*eine gute Frau* / a good woman
dat.	*einem neuen Hut* / to a new hat	*einer guten Frau* / to a good woman
gen.	*eines neuen Hutes* / of a new hat	*einer guten Frau* / of a good woman

Case	Neuter Singular	Plural
nom.	ein alt**es** Radio / an old radio	meine neu**en** Hüte / my new hats
acc.	ein alt**es** Radio / an old radio	deine gut**en** Frauen / your good women
dat.	einem alt**en** Radio / to an old radio	seinen alt**en** Radios / to his old radios
gen.	eines alt**en** Radios / of an old radio	eurer alt**en** Radios / of your old radios

EXAMPLES:

Ich kaufe ihr einen neuen Hut. / I buy her a new hat.
Sie ist eine nette Frau. / She is a nice woman.
Er kommt mit einem neuen Radio. / He comes with a new radio
Haben Sie keine neuen Zeitungen? / Have you no new newspapers?
Das sind die Puppen unsrer kleinen Mädchen. / These are the dolls of our little girls.

§6.1 – 4 Adjectives Used as Nouns

Whenever an adjective is used as a noun, it is declined like an adjective that precedes a noun.

Adjective	Adjective Used as Noun	Meaning
blond	die Blonde	the blonde
verwandt	der Verwandte	the relative
	ein Verwandter	a relative

- Adjectives used as nouns have the same endings whether preceded by „*der*" or „*ein*" words (see §6.1 – 1 and §6.1 – 3) *except* in the nominative masculine, the nominative neuter, and the accusative neuter of the „*ein*" words.

  EXAMPLES:
  Ich bringe der Blonden Blumen. / I bring flowers to the blonde.
  Er ist ein Bekannter von mir. / He is an acquaintance of mine.
  Das ist unser Neuestes. / This is our newest.

- Adjectives following words like *etwas* (something), *nichts* (nothing), *viel* (much), or *wenig* (little) take the neuter singular and are always capitalized.

  EXAMPLES:
  Er verspricht mir etwas Gutes. / He promises me something good.
  Heute singt sie nichts Neues. / Today she sings nothing new.
  Er wünschte ihr viel Gutes. / He wished her all the best.
  Sie erzählte uns wenig Schönes. / She told us little that was nice

**§6.1 – 5
Predicate
Adjectives**

A *predicate adjective* stands after linking verbs like *sein* (to be), *haben* (to have), or *finden* (to find). It states something about the subject of the sentence. It never takes an ending.

EXAMPLES:
Die Schuhe sind teuer. / The shoes are expensive.
Die Frau wird alt. / The woman is getting old.
Er findet das Bild schön. / He finds the picture beautiful.

**§6.1 – 6
Miscellaneous**

• Adjectives ending in *-el* and *-er* lose the *e* when declined.

EXAMPLES:
dunkel / dark   *die dunkle Nacht* / the dark night
teuer / expensive   *der teure Schmuck* / the expensive jewelry

• The adjective *hoch* / high loses the *c* when declined:

der hohe Preis / the high price

**§6.2
COMPARISON
OF
ADJECTIVES**

**§6.2 – 1
Comparative
and
Superlative**

As in English, German adjectives have *comparative* and *superlative* forms. The comparative of an adjective is formed by adding *-er* to its stem (or *-r* if it ends in an *e*); the superlative is formed by adding *-st, or -est* if the adjective ends in *-d, -t, -s, -ß,* or *z.*

Adjective	Comparative	Superlative	Meaning
billig	*billiger*	*billigst*	cheap / cheaper / cheapest
leise	*leiser*	*leisest*	low / lower / lowest
gesund	*gesünder*	*gesündest*	healthy / healthier / healthiest
fett	*fetter*	*fettest*	fat / fatter / fattest
heiß	*heißer*	*heißest*	hot / hotter / hottest
kurz	*kürzer*	*kürzest*	short / shorter / shortest

• Adjectives ending in *-el* always shed the *e* in the comparative:

dunkel, dunkler, dunkelst / dark / darker / darkest

- Many adjectives of one syllable take the umlaut.

Adjective	Comparative	Superlative	Meaning
alt	*älter*	*ältest*	old / older / oldest
arm	*ärmer*	*ärmst*	poor / poorer / poorest
grob	*gröber*	*gröbst*	coarse / coarser / coarsest
hart	*härter*	*härtest*	hard / harder / hardest
jung	*jünger*	*jüngst*	young / younger / youngest
kalt	*kälter*	*kältest*	cold / colder / coldest
klug	*klüger*	*klügst*	clever / cleverer / cleverest
lang	*länger*	*längst*	long / longer / longest
scharf	*schärfer*	*schärfst*	sharp / sharper / sharpest
schwach	*schwächer*	*schwächst*	weak / weaker / weakest
stark	*stärker*	*stärkst*	strong / stronger / strongest
warm	*wärmer*	*wärmst*	warm / warmer / warmest

- A few adjectives have irregular forms.

Adjective	Comparative	Superlative	Meaning
groß	*größer*	*größt*	big / bigger / biggest
hoch	*höher*	*höchst*	high / higher / highest
nah(e)	*näher*	*nächst*	near / nearer / nearest
gut	*besser*	*best*	good / better / best
viel	*mehr*	*meist*	much / more / most

- Comparative and superlative forms are used like any other adjectives, taking the identical endings.

Höhere Berge sind gefährlicher. / Higher mountains are more dangerous.

Er schreibt jetzt für bessere Zeitschriften. / He now writes for better periodicals.

Das sind schärfere Messer. / These are sharper knives.

Mehr ist nicht immer besser. / More is not always better.

Er ist unser bester Student. / He is our best student.

London ist die größte Stadt, die ich kenne. / London is the largest city that I know.
Das ist mein jüngstes Kind. / This is my youngest child.
Wir lernen die schwersten Aufgaben. / We learn the hardest lessons.

- When the superlative is used as a predicate adjective, it takes a different form which does not vary in gender or number.

EXAMPLES:

Diese Kleider sind am teuersten. / These clothes are the most expensive.
Diese Hemden sind am billigsten. / These shirts are the cheapest.

§6.2–2 Positive

The *positive* degree is used to compare people or things of equal value.

EXAMPLES:

Ich bin (eben)so gescheit wie er. / I am just *as* smart *as* he.
Er ist so groß wie ich. / He is *as* tall *as* I.

When comparing an inequality, the word **als** (than) is used.

EXAMPLES:

Ich gehe schneller als er. / I walk faster *than* he.
Der Ring kostet mehr als die Uhr. / The ring costs more *than* the watch.

§6.3 Possessive Adjectives

There is a group of *possessive adjectives* that are actually possessive pronouns used as adjectives whenever they precede a noun:

mein (my), *dein* (your), *Ihr* (your — formal), *sein* (his), *ihr* (her), *unser* (our), *euer* (your), *Ihr* (your — formal), *ihr* (their).

EXAMPLES:

mein Vater / my father
seine Mutter / his mother

You will find a discussion of these forms in §7.2.

§7.

Pronouns

A *pronoun* is a word that replaces a noun or a noun phrase, refers back to it, or inquires after it.

- Personal pronouns

> *Der Mann ist reich. **Er** ist auch freigebig.* / The man is rich. He also is generous.

The word *er* is a *personal pronoun;* it replaces the subject noun *Mann.*

- Reflexive pronouns

> *Der Junge wäscht **sich**.* / The boy washes himself.

The word *sich* is a *reflexive pronoun;* it refers back to the subject noun *Junge.*

- Possessive pronouns

> *Fritz liest **mein** Buch.* / Fritz is reading my book.

The word *mein* preceding the noun, is a *possessive pronoun* used as a *possessive adjective.*

> *Das Buch ist **mein**.* / The book is mine.

The word *mein,* standing by itself, is a *possessive pronoun;* it replaces the name of the possessor.

- Demonstrative pronouns

> ***Dieser (der)** Junge ist nett.* / This boy is nice

The words *dieser* and *der* are *demonstrative pronouns,* used as *demonstrative adjectives.*

> ***Der** ist nett.* / He (This one) is nice.

The word *der,* standing by itself, is used as a *demonstrative pronoun;* it replaces the noun. Demonstratives were included and discussed in the section on Articles (see Chapter 5).

- Relative pronouns

> *Das Mädchen, **das** dort steht, ist meine Schwester.* /
> The girl that is standing there is my sister.

The word *das* (the second *das*) is a *relative pronoun;* it refers back to the noun in the main clause.

- Interrogative pronouns

> ***Wessen** Bleistift ist das?* / Whose pencil is this?

The word *wessen* is an interrogative pronoun; it inquires after a person or thing.

- Indefinite pronouns

> *Hier darf **man** nicht rauchen.* / One must not smoke here.

In the sentence above, the word *man* is an indefinite pronoun; it replaces a noun subject, a person, or persons who are not clearly defined. *Etwas* / something, replaces a thing or an object. The different types of pronouns will be discussed in the sections below.

§7.1 PERSONAL PRONOUNS

Personal pronouns refer to living beings, objects, or ideas. The first person is used by a speaker or writer about himself or herself (*ich, wir* / I, we). The second person is the person spoken or written to (*du, ihr, Sie* / you). The third person is the person or thing spoken or written about (*er, sie, es; sie* / he, she, it, they).

§7.1–1 Subject

Subject pronouns are used in the nominative. They have the following forms:

	Person	German Forms	English Equivalent	Examples
S i n g u l a r	1st	*ich*	I	*Ich bin zufrieden.* / I am satisfied.
	2nd	*du* *Sie*	you (familiar) you (formal)	*Lernst du Deutsch?* / Are you learning German? *Kommen Sie?* / Are you coming?
	3rd	*er* *sie* *es*	he she it	*Er spricht gut.* / He speaks well. *Sie ist nett.* / She is nice. *Es schneit.* / It is snowing.

	Person	German Forms	English Equivalent	Examples
P l u r a l	1st	*wir*	we	*Wir gehen weg.* / We go away.
	2nd	*ihr*	you (familiar)	*Wo seid ihr?* / Where are you?
		Sie	you (formal)	*Wo wohnen Sie?* / Where do you live?
	3rd	*sie*	they	*Sie sind hier.* / They are here.

- The pronoun *ich* (I) is never capitalized unless it is the first word of a sentence.
- The familiar forms *du* and *ihr* are used when addressing members of the family, children, or close friends.
- *Sie* (capitalized) is more formal. Because capitalization is the only thing that differentiates *Sie* (you) from the third person plural *sie* (they), some grammars list them together. Nevertheless, *Sie* (you) is both singular and plural, second person, and has been listed here as such.

EXAMPLES:

*Siehst **du** das, Mutter?* / Do you see that, Mother?
*Karl und Franz, habt **ihr** das Geschirr gewaschen?* / Karl and Franz, did you wash the dishes?
*Herr Schmidt, haben **Sie** das gelesen?* / Herr Schmidt, did you read this?
*Meine Herren, sind **Sie** damit einverstanden?* / Gentlemen, do you agree with this?

§7.1–2
Object

Object Pronouns in the Accusative

Object pronouns are used in the accusative as direct objects or as objects of a preposition that takes the accusative. They have the following forms:

	Person	German Form	English Equivalent	Examples
S i n g u l a r	1st	*mich*	me	*Karl ruft mich.* / Karl calls me.
	2nd	*dich*	you (familiar)	*Er braucht dich.* / He needs you.
		Sie	you (formal)	*Wir besuchen Sie.* / We visit you.
	3rd	*ihn*	him	*Eva liebt ihn.* / Eva loves him.
		sie	her	*Paul liebt sie.* / Paul loves her.
		es	it	*Hans kauft es.* / Hans buys it.
P l u r a l	1st	*uns*	us	*Sie sieht uns.* / She sees us.
	2nd	*euch*	you (familiar)	*Kurt sieht euch.* / Kurt sees you.
		Sie	you (formal	*Ich höre Sie.* / I hear you.
	3rd	*sie*	them	*Nora wäscht sie.* / Nora washes them.

EXAMPLES:

Wo triffst du **mich** *heute?* / Where are you meeting me today?
Ich höre **ihn** *sehr gut.* / I hear him very well.
Wir sehen **Sie** *morgen, Herr Schmidt.* / We will see you
   tomorrow, *Mr. Schmidt.*
Ich liebe **sie** *beide.* / I love them both.
Hans besucht **uns** *morgen.* / Hans will visit us tomorrow.

Object Pronouns in the Dative

Object pronouns are used in the dative as indirect objects
or as objects of a preposition that takes the dative. They
have the following forms:

Person	German Form	English Equivalent	Examples
1st	*mir*	to me	*Karl kommt zu mir.* / Karl comes to me.
2nd	*dir*	to you (familiar)	*Das gehört dir.* / That belongs to you.
	Ihnen	to you (formal)	*Otto schreibt Ihnen.* / Otto writes to you.
3rd	*ihm (m.)*	to him	*Das Buch gehört ihm.* / Tl ̖ ̗ook belongs to him.
	ihr (f.)	to her	*Ich fahre zu ihr.* / I drive to her.
	ihm (n.)	to it	*Gib ihm (dem Pferd) Wasser!* / Give it (the horse) some water.
1st	*uns*	to us	*Paul spricht zu uns.* / Paul speaks to us.
2nd	*euch*	to you (familiar)	*Schreibt euch das Kind?* / Does the child write you?
	Ihnen	to you (formal)	*Fritz fährt zu Ihnen.* / Fritz is driving to you.
3rd	*ihnen*	to them	*Er gibt ihnen das Geld.* / He gives the money to them.

(Left margin: S i n g u l a r / P l u r a l)

EXAMPLES:

Er gibt **mir** *etwas.* / He gives me something.
Er kommt zu **euch.** / He comes to you.
Das gehört **Ihnen,** Herr Müller / That belongs to you, Mr. Müller.
Das gehört **ihm,** dem Sohn. / That belongs to him, the son.
Das gehört **ihr,** der Tochter. / That belongs to her, the daughter.
Das gehört **ihm,** dem Mädchen. / That belongs to her, the girl.
Das gehört **ihm,** dem Tier. / That belongs to it, the animal.

Note: The word *Mädchen* (girl) is a neuter noun.

7.1–3
Reflexive

A *reflexive pronoun* "reflects" or refers back to the subject:

Ich wasche mich. / I wash myself. German does not distinguish
reflexive pronouns from object pronouns by the use of "self"
(as we do in English). The only exclusively reflexive pronoun
is *sich*, used with the formal you (*Sie*), singular and plural,
and with all third person forms. *Sich* is both accusative and
dative. Otherwise, object pronouns, accusative or dative, do
double duty as reflexive pronouns.

Reflexive Pronouns in the Accusative

Reflexive pronouns in the accusative take the same forms as the corresponding object pronouns, except in the second person formal and in the third person.

	Person	German Form	English Equivalent	Examples
S i n g u l a r	1st	*mich*	myself	*Ich rasiere mich.* / I shave myself.
	2nd	*dich* *sich*	yourself (familiar) yourself (formal)	*Du schneidest dich.* / You cut yourself. *Sie schneiden sich.* / You cut yourself.
	3rd	*sich*	himself herself itself	*Er verletzt sich.* / He hurts himself. *Sie kämmt sich.* / She combs herself. *Es (das Kind) wäscht sich.* / It (the child) washes itself.
P l u r a l	1st	*uns*	ourselves	*Wir waschen uns.* / We wash ourselves.
	2nd	*euch* *sich*	yourselves (familiar) yourselves (formal)	*Ihr kämmt euch.* / You comb yourselves. *Sie kämmen sich.* / You comb yourselves.
	3rd	*sich*	themselves	*Sie kämmen sich.* / They comb themselves.

Some reflexive forms in German have nonreflexive forms in English.

EXAMPLES:
*Er fürchtet **sich** vor dem Donner.* / He is afraid of thunder.
*Wir freuen **uns** auf Ostern.* / We look forward to Easter.
*Ihr erinnert **euch** daran.* / You remember (remind yourself of) it
*Sie weigern **sich**, es zu tun.* / They refuse to do it.
*Sie hat **sich** versprochen.* / She made a slip of the tongue.
*Er hat **sich** verlaufen.* / He lost his way.
*Ich habe **mich** erkältet.* / I caught a cold.

Reflexive Pronouns in the Dative

Reflexive pronouns in the dative take the same forms as corresponding object pronouns in the first person and second person familiar. In the second person formal and in the third person, they have the same form as reflexive pronouns in the accusative.

EXAMPLES:
*Ich gefalle **mir** sehr gut.* / I like myself very much.
*Du hast **dir** wehgetan.* / You have hurt yourself.
*Er hat **sich** ein Buch gekauft.* / He bought himself a book.
*Wir nehmen **uns** Geld mit.* / We take money along (for ourselves
*Ihr holt **euch** die Zeitung.* / You get the paper (for yourselves).

Sie machen es **sich** *gemütlich.* / They make themselves comfortable.
Herr Schmidt, haben Sie **sich** *das Taxi bestellt?* / Mr. Schmidt, did you order the cab for yourself?

In German some sentences referring to parts of the body or to clothing use reflexive pronouns.

EXAMPLES:
Ich wasche **mir** *das Gesicht.* / I wash my face.
Ich putze **mir** *die Zähne.* / I brush my teeth.
Ich kämme **mir** *das Haar.* / I comb my hair.
Ich ziehe **mir** *das Kleid an.* / I put on my dress.
Ich setze **mir** *die Kappe auf.* / I put on my cap.

The Reflexive Pronouns *einander* and *gegenseitig*

In the sentence *Sie rissen* **sich** *die Haare aus* (They tore out their hair), it is unclear whether each person tore out his own hair or if each tore out the hair of the other. If the latter is true, the sentence should be changed to:

Sie rissen einander die Haare aus.

OR

Sie rissen sich gegenseitig die Haare aus. / They tore out each other's hair.

Other uses of *einander* (when combined with a preposition) are:

Sie verliebten sich ineinander. / They fell in love with each other.
Sie schämen sich voreinander. / They are ashamed of each other.
Die Männer streiten miteinander. / The men fight with each other.

§7.2 POSSESSIVES

Possessives denote ownership. Their use generally corresponds to English usage. Each possessive can be used as an adjective or as an independent pronoun.

● The declension of the possessive adjective in the singular follows the pattern of the indefinite article *ein* (see §5.3). The declension of the possessive adjective in the plural follows the pattern of the demonstrative *diese* (see §5.4).

EXAMPLES:

Indefinite Article	Singular Possessive Adjective
ein Mann / a man	*mein Mann* / my man (husband)
eine Frau / a woman	*meine Frau* / my woman (wife)
ein Kind / a child	*mein Kind* / my child

Demonstrative (same for all genders)	Plural Possessive Adjective
diese Kinder / these children	*meine Kinder* / my children

POSSESSIVE ADJECTIVES

Case	Singular Masculine	Feminine	Neuter	Plural	Meaning
nom.	mein	meine	mein	meine	my
acc.	meinen	meine	mein	meine	my
dat.	meinem	meiner	meinem	meinen	to my
gen.	meines	meiner	meines	meiner	of my
nom.	dein	deine	dein	deine	your
acc.	deinen	deine	dein	deine	your
dat.	deinem	deiner	deinem	deinen	to your
gen.	deines	deiner	deines	deiner	of your
nom.	sein	seine	sein	seine	his
acc.	seinen	seine	sein	seine	his
dat.	seinem	seiner	seinem	seinen	to his
gen.	seines	seiner	seines	seiner	of his
nom.	ihr	ihre	ihr	ihre	her
acc.	ihren	ihre	ihr	ihre	her
dat.	ihrem	ihrer	ihrem	ihren	to her
gen.	ihres	ihrer	ihres	ihrer	of her

POSSESSIVE ADJECTIVES

Case	Singular Masculine	Feminine	Neuter	Plural	Meaning
nom.	unser	uns(e)re	unser	uns(e)re	our
acc.	uns(e)ren	uns(e)re	unser	uns(e)re	our
dat.	uns(e)rem	uns(e)rer	uns(e)rem	uns(e)re	to our
gen.	uns(e)res	uns(e)rer	uns(e)res	uns(e)rer	of our
nom.	euer	eure	euer	eure	your
acc.	euren	eure	euer	eure	your
dat.	eurem	eurer	eurem	euren	to your
gen.	eures	eurer	eures	eurer	of your
nom.	ihr	ihre	ihr	ihre	their
acc.	ihren	ihre	ihr	ihre	their
dat.	ihrem	ihrer	ihrem	ihren	to their
gen.	ihres	ihrer	ihres	ihrer	of their
nom.	Ihr	Ihre	Ihr	Ihre	your
acc.	Ihren	Ihre	Ihr	Ihre	your
dat.	Ihrem	Ihrer	Ihrem	Ihren	to your
gen.	Ihres	Ihrer	Ihres	Ihrer	of your

- The rules for spelling irregularities are as follows: *unser* and *euer* lose the -*e*- of the stem whenever the ending starts with -*e*. However, the full forms can also be used: *unseren, unsere, eueren, euerem,* etc., but never *euerer.*

  EXAMPLES:

  Meine Schwester ist hübsch. / My sister is pretty.
  Ich habe deinen Bleistift. / I have your pencil.
  Er hilft seinem Vater. / He helps his father.
  Ich mag die Farbe ihres Kleides. / I like the color of her dress.
  Sie braucht deine Hilfe. / She needs your help.
  Er spricht mit eurer Mutter. / He speaks with your mother.
  Hast du unsren Lehrer gesehen? / Did you see our teacher?
  Er besucht Ihren Onkel. / He visits your uncle.

- A *possessive pronoun* must stand by itself and not precede a noun. If preceded by the definite article, it follows the adjective declension with weak endings (see §6.1 – 1).

  EXAMPLES:

  Hier ist mein Buch. Wo ist das deine? / Here is my book.
  Where is yours?
  Hat er seinen Kugelschreiber verloren? Gib ihm den meinen.
  Did he lose his ball-point pen? Give him mine.

- If the possessive pronoun is used without an article, it usually follows the declensional endings of *dieser* (see §5.4).

  EXAMPLES:

  Hier ist ein Mantel. Ist es deiner? / Here is a coat. Is it yours?
  Hier ist ein Wörterbuch. Ist es eures? Ich habe meines bei mir. / Here is a dictionary. Is it yours? I have mine with me.

- If the possessive pronoun is used as a predicate nominative with the verbs *sein, werden,* or *bleiben,* it takes no endings.

  EXAMPLES:

  Er ist mein und bleibt mein. / He is mine and remains mine.
  Der Sieg ist unser. / The victory is ours.
  Der Ring wird morgen dein. / The ring will be yours tomorrow.

7.3
RELATIVE
PRONOUNS

A *relative pronoun* introduces a relative clause by referring to a noun or pronoun in the preceding main clause. The element to which the relative pronoun refers is called the *antecedent.*

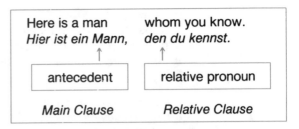

The relative pronouns in German are *der/die/das* (who, that, which), *wer/was* (who, that), and *welcher* (who, that). Their use depends on the context of the sentence.

The relative pronouns *der/die/das* are declined as follows

	Case	Masculine	Feminine	Neuter	Meaning
S i n g u l a r	nom.	der	die	das	that, who, which
	acc.	den	die	das	that, who, which
	dat.	dem	der	dem	to whom, to which
	gen.	dessen	deren	dessen	whose, of which
P l u r a l	nom.	die	Same for all three genders.		that, who, which
	acc.	die			that, who, which
	dat.	denen			to whom, to which
	gen.	deren			of whom, of which

- The gender as well as the number of the relative pronoun agrees with the gender and the number of its antecedent. The case of the relative pronoun is determined by its use or function within the relative clause.

  EXAMPLES:
  Kennen Sie den Mann, der hier wohnt? / Do you know the man who lives here?
  Brauchen Sie das Buch, das ich Ihnen lieh? / Do you need the book that I lent you?
  Dort sind meine Eltern, bei denen ich wohne. / There are my parents, with whom I live.
  Das ist das Mädchen, dessen Haar ich bewundere. / That is the girl whose hair I admire.

- The combination of *wo(r)-* with a preposition often replaces the relative pronoun.

EXAMPLES:

*Hier ist das Haus, **in dem** ich wohne.*

OR

*Hier ist das Haus, **worin** ich wohne.* / Here is the house in
which I live.

*Das ist der Bleistift, **mit dem** ich schreibe.*

OR

*Das ist der Bleistift, **womit** ich schreibe.* / That is the pencil
with which I write.

• *Wo* (where) may be used by itself, instead of a preposition
plus a relative pronoun.

EXAMPLES:

*Das ist die Straße, **auf der** wir spielten.* / That is the street on
which we played.

OR

*Das ist die Straße, **wo** wir spielten.* / That is the street where
we played.

Note that the relative clause is always separated from
the main clause by a comma.

• The pronoun *wer* relates to a person or persons who are
not clearly defined.

EXAMPLE:

***Wer** viel studiert, bekommt gute Noten.* / He who studies much
gets good grades.

• If the antecedent is an indefinite pronoun (see §7.5) or an
adjective used as a neuter noun (*das Netteste* / the nicest),
the relative pronoun **was** can be used.

EXAMPLES:

*Du hast etwas getan, **was** häßlich ist.* / You did something that
is ugly.

*Er weiß nichts, **was** wichtig ist.* / He knows nothing that is
important.

*Ist das das Netteste, **was** Sie haben?* / Is that the nicest that
you have?

• The relative pronoun *welcher* takes the same declension as
the words *dieser* or *jener* (§5.4). It has no genitive form.
Compared with the relative pronouns *der/die/das*, its use
is quite limited. It is used primarily for stylistic reasons (such
as to avoid repetition).

EXAMPLES:

*Sind Sie die, **welche** heute anfängt?*

INSTEAD OF

*Sind Sie die, **die** heute anfängt?* / **Are you the one who starts today?**

*Er sprach mit dem Kind, **welches** das Geld verloren hatte.*

INSTEAD OF

*Er sprach mit dem Kind, **das** das Geld verloren hatte.* / **He spoke to the child who had lost the money.**

§7.4 INTER-ROGATIVE PRONOUNS

An *interrogative pronoun* replaces a noun or noun phrase introducing a question. The main German interrogative pronouns are *wer* (who), *was* (what), and *welcher* (which).

FORMS OF *WER* AND *WAS*			
Case	Masculine and Feminine	Neuter	Meaning
nom.	*wer*	*was*	who, what
acc.	*wen*	*was*	whom, what
dat.	*wem*	—	to whom
gen.	*wessen*	*wessen*	whose

EXAMPLES:

***Wer** ist da?* / **Who is here?**
***Wen** sehe ich dort?* / **Whom do I see there?**
***Wem** soll ich das geben?* / **To whom shall I give that?**
***Wessen** Schuhe sind das?* / **Whose shoes are these?**
***Was** ist auf dem Tisch?* / **What is on the table?**
***Was** tust du?* / **What are you doing?**

Note that there are no separate forms for the masculine and feminine, and there are no plural forms.

• Word combinations with the prefixes *wo-* or *wor-* can be used instead of *was.*

Avoid	Use instead
Mit was schreibst du?	**Womit** schreibst du? / **With what are you writing?**
Für was ist das gut?	**Wofür** ist das gut? / **What is this good for?**
An was denkst du?	**Woran** denkst du? / **What are you thinking about?**
Auf was wartet er?	**Worauf** wartet er? / **What is he waiting for?**
Von was spricht er?	**Wovon** spricht er? / **What is he talking about?**

Note: *wo-* combinations cannot be used when referring to people:

Auf wen wartest du? / For whom are you waiting?

The interrogative *welcher* can be used as an adjective or as a pronoun.

FORMS OF *WELCHER*

Case	Masculine	Feminine	Neuter	Meaning
nom.	welcher	welche	welches	which, which one
acc.	welchen	welche	welches	which, which one
dat.	welchem	welcher	welchem	to which, to which one
gen.	welchen	welcher	welchen	of which, of which one
nom.	welche	Same for all three genders.		which, which ones
acc.	welche			which, which ones
dat.	welchen			to which, to which ones
gen.	welcher			of which, of which ones

- The form *welches* is used for masculine nouns ending in *-en* in the genitive singular.

  EXAMPLE:
  Welches Menschen? / Of which human being?"

- *Welcher* can be used as an interrogative adjective.

  EXAMPLES:
  Ruth hat viele Kleider. / Ruth has many dresses.
  Welches Kleid hat sie am liebsten? / Which dress does she like best?
  Welche Kleider mag sie nicht? / Which dresses does she not like?

- Or it can be used as an interrogative pronoun.

  EXAMPLES:
  Ich habe hier drei Platten. / I have here three records.
  Welche wollen Sie kaufen? / Which one(s) do you want to buy?
  Welche haben Sie schon gehört? / Which one(s) have you heard already?

- *Kein* is the negative form of the indefinite article *ein.* It indicates the absence of a person or an object. But unlike *ein,* it does have all plural forms, and takes the endings of the definite article *der* (see §5.2).

Case	Singular			Plural	Meaning
	Masculine	**Feminine**	**Neuter**	**All Genders**	
nom.	*kein*	*keine*	*kein*	*keine*	no, not any, none
acc.	*keinen*	*keine*	*kein*	*keine*	no, not any, none
dat.	*keinem*	*keiner*	*keinem*	*keinen*	to none
gen.	*keines*	*keiner*	*keines*	*keiner*	of none

Kein used as an indefinite adjective:

Er hat keine Zeit. / He has no time.
Wir haben keine Bananen. / We have no bananas.
Er ist Mitglied keiner Partei. / He is a member of no party.

Kein used as an indefinite pronoun:

Keiner von ihnen ist gekommen. / None of them came.
Das tut keiner. / Nobody does that.

§7.5 INDEFINITE PRONOUNS

Indefinite pronouns refer to persons or objects that the speaker cannot or will not identify. A majority of them can also be used as indefinite adjectives.

EXAMPLES:

Indefinite Adjectives	Indefinite Pronouns
alle Bücher / all books	*Alle sind weg.* / All are gone.
ein anderes Mal / another time	*Ein anderer kam.* / Another one came.
einige (mehrere) Leute / some (several) people	*einige (mehrere) blieben.* / Some (several) remained.
jede Frau / each woman	*Jeder hilft.* / Everybody is helping.

IMPORTANT INDEFINITE PRONOUNS

Indefinite Stem	For People	For Objects	Meaning
all-	*alle*	*alle(s)*	all
ander-	*andere(r)*	*andere(s)*	other
einig-	*einige*	*einige(s)*	some
etwas	—	*etwas*	something
jed-	*jede(r)*	*jedes*	each, every, everybody
jemand	*jemand*	—	somebody
kein-	*keine(r)*	*keine(s)*	no, not any, none, nobody
man	*man*	—	one, they, people
mehrer-	*mehrere*	*mehrere(s)*	several
nichts	—	*nichts*	nothing
niemand	*niemand*	—	nobody

- The words *etwas* and *nichts* have no declension; *jemand* and *niemand* usually are not declined in colloquial speech.
- The word *man* always refers to people; it occurs in the nominative only. For the other cases forms of *ein-* are used.

  EXAMPLES

  Man spielt heute Hamlet. / Today they play Hamlet.
  Das freut einen. / That pleases one.
  Sie lassen einem keine Zeit. / They don't allow one time.

Verbs

Verbs are words that describe an action, a process, or a state of being. Verbs agree with the person of the subject (first, second, or third person) and with its number (singular or plural).

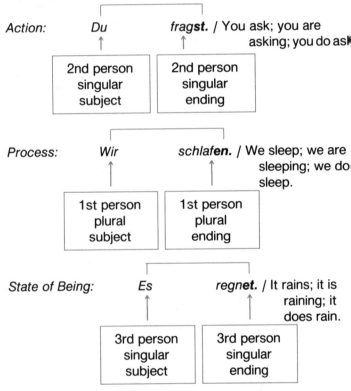

Action: *Du*   *frag**st**.* / You ask; you are asking; you do ask

| 2nd person singular subject | 2nd person singular ending |

Process: *Wir*   *schlafen.* / We sleep; we are sleeping; we do sleep.

| 1st person plural subject | 1st person plural ending |

State of Being: *Es*   *regn**et**.* / It rains; it is raining; it does rain.

| 3rd person singular subject | 3rd person singular ending |

- German verbs are listed in the dictionary in their *infinitive* form. Except for *sein* (to be), *tun* (to do), and a few verbs ending in *-eln* (*betteln* / to beg) and *-ern* (*erobern* / to conquer, see §8.2-1), the infinitives of German verbs end in *-e*

  fragen / to ask
  schlafen / to sleep
  regnen / to rain

- The *stems* of these verbs are *frag-, schlaf-,* and *regn-.*

  When verbs are conjugated, they change their form to show tense (present tense, past tense, present perfect, etc.), mood (indicative, subjunctive), person, number, and voice (active and passive).

In German, there are "weak" verbs, which do not change the stem vowel in the past tense and the past participle; "strong" verbs, which do change their stem vowels in these tenses; and irregular verbs, which have features of both weak and strong verbs.

§8.2
THE INDICATIVE MOOD

The *indicative mood* expresses or "indicates" facts. It is used to make statements, exchange information, etc.

§8.2–1
Present Tense

Weak Verbs

The present tense of *weak verbs* is formed as follows:

• Drop the infinitive ending of the verb and add the following endings to the stem:

	Person	Endings	Example	Meaning
Si**n**g**u**l**a**r	1st	-e	*ich frage*	I ask
	2nd	-st (familiar)	*du fragst*	you ask
		-en (formal)	*Sie fragen*	you ask
	3rd *(m.)*	-t	*er fragt*	he asks
	(f.)	-t	*sie fragt*	she asks
	(n.)	-t	*es fragt*	it asks
Pl**u**r**a**l	1st	-en	*wir fragen*	we ask
	2nd	-t (familiar) -en (formal)	*ihr fragt* *Sie fragen*	you ask you ask
	3rd	-en	*sie fragen*	they ask

Note: In the conjugation tables that follow, the third person masculine singular will stand also for the feminine and neuter forms: *er (sie, es) fragt* / he (she, it) asks. The second person formal singular is always identical to the second person formal plural. Both of these forms are identical to the third person plural.

- If the stem of the verb ends in -d, -t, -m, or -n, the vowel -e is inserted in the second and third person singular and in the second person plural:

  du findest / you find
  er arbeitet / he works
  ihr atmet / you breathe
  er zeichnet / he draws

  BUT

  er filmt / he films
  du lernst / you learn

- If the stem of the verb ends in -s, -ß, -x, or -z, the -s- in the ending of the second person singular is omitted:

  du rast / you speed
  du haßt / you hate
  du mixt / you mix
  du setzt / you put

- If the stem of the verb ends in -eln, the -e- is dropped in the first person singular, as in the verbs *klingeln* (to ring), *lächeln* (to smile), and *sammeln* (to collect):

  ich klingle / I ring
  ich lächle / I smile
  ich sammle / I collect

- If the stem of the verb ends in -eln or -ern, the ending for the first and third person plural is -n; they have the same form as the infinitive:

  wir lächeln / we smile
  sie ändern / they change

Examples of Weak Verbs in the Present Tense

Er findet das Buch. / He finds the book.
Arbeitest du schwer? / Do you work hard?
Zeichnest du einen Baum? / Do you draw a tree?
Du rast doch wie ein Verrückter! / You speed like a madman.
Warum setzt du dich nicht? / Why don't you sit down?
Ich sammle Briefmarken. / I collect postage stamps.
Wir lächeln darüber. / We smile about it.

Strong Verbs

In the present tense, *strong verbs* change their stem vowel as follows:

- Strong verbs with the stem vowel -a- change it to -ä- in the second and third person singular:

ich fahre / I drive   ich schlafe / I sleep
du fährst / you drive   du schläfst / you sleep
er fährt / he drives   er schläft / he sleeps

- Those with the stem vowel -e- change it to -i- or -ie-:

ich gebe / I give   ich lese / I read
du gibst / you give du liest / you read
er gibt / he gives   er liest / he reads

Note the following changes in spelling:

ich esse / I eat   ich nehme / I take
du ißt / you eat   du nimmst / you take
er ißt / he eats   er nimmt / he takes

- The verbs *gehen* (to go) and *stehen* (to stand) have an -e- vowel in the stem, but they *do not* change it:

ich gehe / I go   ich stehe / I stand
du gehst / you go   du stehst / you stand
er geht / he goes   er steht / he stands

- The verbs *wissen* (to know) and *tun* (to do) are irregular in the singular and plural:

ich weiß / I know   ich tu(e) / I do
du weißt / you know   du tust / you do
er weiß / he knows   er tut / he does
wir wissen / we know   wir tun / we do
ihr wißt / you know   ihr tut / you do
sie wissen / they know   sie tun / they do

Examples of Strong Verbs in the Present Tense

Schläfst du, wenn du fährst? / Do you sleep when you drive?
Er gibt ihm Geld. / He gives him money.
Sie ißt ihr Frühstück. / She eats her breakfast.
Du nimmst die Zeitung. / You take the paper.
Gehst du ins Kino? / Do you go to the movies?
Wo steht er? / Where is he standing?
Weißt du das nicht? / Don't you know that?
Wir tun das nicht. / We don't do that.

Continued Action

When expressing a situation that started in the past and continues into the present, we use the present perfect in English and the present tense in German.

EXAMPLES:
Ich arbeite schon drei Jahre für diese Firma. / I have been working for this firm for three years.

Ich bin schon seit zwei Tagen hier. / I have been here for two days.

Note: The time phrase is usually accompanied by *schon* (already), *seit* (since), or by *schon seit* — telltale signs of continued action.

Auxiliary Verbs

There are three auxiliary (or helping) verbs in German: the verbs *sein* (to be), *haben* (to have), and *werden* (to become, get, grow, come to be). The verbs *sein* and *haben* are as commonly used in German as are their equivalents in English. They can be used as words in their own right, but usually they help to form other verb forms. All three verbs are irregular.

sein / to be	
ich bin / I am	*wir sind* / we are
du bist / you are	*ihr seid* / you are
er ist / he is	*sie sind* / they are

EXAMPLES:
Ich bin Lehrer. / I am a teacher.
Bist du zu Hause? / Are you at home?
Wir sind zufrieden. / We are satisfied.

haben / to have	
ich habe / I have	*wir haben* / we have
du hast / you have	*ihr habt* / you have
er hat / he has	*sie haben* / they have

EXAMPLES:
Du hast ein Auto. / You have a car.
Sie hat ein hübsches Kleid. / She has a pretty dress.
Haben Sie einen Computer? / Do you have a computer?

werden / to become, get, grow, come to be	
ich werde / I become	*wir werden* / we become
du wirst / you become	*ihr werdet* / you become
er wird / he becomes	*sie werden* / they become

EXAMPLES:
Er wird Arzt. / He becomes (is becoming) a doctor.
Wirst du böse? / Do you get angry?
Wir werden reich. / We come to be (are getting) rich.

§8.2-2
Past Tense

The *past tense,* also called *imperfect,* is used in German primarily to report or narrate past events, sometimes a recurring or habitual action — especially in written or formal usage.

EXAMPLES:
Voriges Jahr wohnte er in München. / Last year he lived in Munich.
Um sechs Uhr machte er gewöhnlich einen Spaziergang. / At six o'clock he usually went for a walk.

Weak Verbs

The past tense of *weak verbs* is formed by adding the following endings to the verb stem:

	Person	Ending	Example	Meaning
S i n g u l a r	1st 2nd 3rd	-te -test -te	*ich fragte* *du fragtest* *er fragte*	I asked you asked he asked
P l u r a l	1st 2nd 3rd	-ten -tet -ten	*wir fragten* *ihr fragtet* *sie fragten*	we asked you asked they asked

- If the stem of the verb ends in *-d, -t, -m,* or *-n,* the vowel *-e-* is inserted between the stem and the ending.

EXAMPLES:
es blendete / it blinded
du arbeitetest / you worked
wir atmeten / we breathed
sie zeichnete / she drew

BUT

er filmte / he filmed
er lernte / he learned

Strong Verbs

To form the past tense, *strong verbs* change their stem vowels and take the following endings:

nehmen / to take	*fangen* / to catch	*fahren* / to drive
ich nahm / I took	*ich fing* / I caught	*ich fuhr* / I drove
du nahmst / you took	*du fingst* / you caught	*du fuhrst* / you drove
er nahm / he took	*er fing* / he caught	*er fuhr* / he drove
wir nahmen / we took	*wir fingen* / we caught	*wir fuhren* / we drove
ihr nahmt / you took	*ihr fingt* / you caught	*ihr fuhrt* / you drove
sie nahmen / they took	*sie fingen* / they caught	*sie fuhren* / they drove

EXAMPLES:

Wir nahmen Theaterkarten für morgen. / We took theater tickets for tomorrow.
Fingst du den Ball, Peter? / Did you catch the ball, Peter?
Gestern nahm ich das Auto und fuhr nach Rom. / Yesterday I took the car, and drove to Rome.

Note: For an extensive treatment of strong verbs, see §8.2–3.

Irregular Verbs

Irregular verbs change the vowel in the stem and, in addition, take weak verb endings.

Infinitive	Meaning	Past Tense (3rd Person)	Meaning
brennen	to burn	*es brannte*	it burned
kennen	to know	*er kannte*	he knew
nennen	to name	*er nannte*	he named
rennen	to run	*er rannte*	he ran
senden	to send	*er sandte*	he sent
wenden	to turn	*er wandte*	he turned
bringen	to bring	*er brachte*	he brought
denken	to think	*er dachte*	he thought
wissen	to know	*er wußte*	he knew

EXAMPLES:

Kanntest du diesen Mann? / Did you know this man?
Der Wagen rannte gegen die Wand. / The car ran into the wall.
Er brachte mir ein Buch. / He brought me a book.
Dachten Sie an Ihre Mutter? / Did you think of your mother?
Ich wußte das nicht. / I did not know that.

Auxiliary Verbs

sein / to be	
ich war / I was	*wir waren* / we were
du warst / you were	*ihr wart* / you were
er war / he was	*sie waren* / they were
haben / to have	
ich hatte / I had	*wir hatten* / we had
du hattest / you had	*ihr hattet* / you had
er hatte / he had	*sie hatten* / they had
werden / to become	
ich wurde / I became	*wir wurden* / we became
du wurdest / you became	*ihr wurdet* / you became
er wurde / he became	*sie wurden* / they became

EXAMPLES:
Warst du gestern im Kino? / Were you at the movies yesterday?
Wart ihr in der Schule? / Were you in school?
Er hatte eine Erkältung. / He had a cold.
Er wurde Arzt. / He became a doctor.

**8.2–3
Present
Perfect Tense**

Weak Verbs

The *present perfect tense* is the verb form used most frequently in German, next to the present tense. It is the tense commonly used in conversation and is, in most instances, the equivalent of the English past tense.

- The present perfect is formed by taking the present tense of the auxiliary verbs *haben* or *sein* plus the past participle of the main verb.

- Most of the German past participles are formed with *ge-* preceding the stem of the verb. If the verb is weak, the ending is *-t* or *-et*. If strong, the ending is *-en* (see the following section).

EXAMPLE:
Ich   habe   den Mann   gefragt. / I have asked the man.

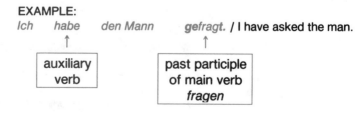

Note: The present participle always stands at the end o
the clause.

EXAMPLES:

Hast du Deutsch gelernt? / Did you learn German?
Wir haben ihn gefragt. / We asked him.
Sie hat viel gearbeitet. / She worked a great deal.

- Weak Verbs ending in *-ieren* do not take the prefix *ge-* in
  the formation of the past participle.

EXAMPLES:

buchstabieren / to spell
Er hat mir das Wort buchstabiert. / He spelled the word for me
reparieren / to repair
Haben Sie die Schuhe repariert? / Did you repair the shoes?
marschieren / to march
Die Soldaten haben die ganze Nacht marschiert. / The
soldiers marched all night.

Auxiliary Verbs

sein / to be	
ich bin gewesen / I have been	*wir sind gewesen* / we have been
du bist gewesen / you have been	*ihr seid gewesen* / you have been
er ist gewesen / he has been	*sie sind gewesen* / they have been

haben / to have	
ich habe gehabt / I have had	*wir haben gehabt* / we have had
du hast gehabt / you have had	*ihr habt gehabt* / you have had
er hat gehabt / he has had	*sie haben gehabt* / they have had

werden / to become	
ich bin geworden / I have become	*wir sind geworden* / we have become
du bist geworden / you have become	*ihr seid geworden* / you have become
er ist geworden / he has become	*sie sind geworden* / they have become

EXAMPLES:

Wir sind heute zu Hause gewesen. / We have been (were) at
home today.
Ist er im Konzert gewesen? / Has he been (Was he) at the
concert?
Hast du die Prüfung gehabt? / Did you have (Have you had) the
exam?

Ist dein Bruder Rechtsanwalt geworden? / Did your brother (Has your brother) become a lawyer?

Strong Verbs

There are groups of strong verbs that change the stem vowel of the infinitive to form the past tense and the past participle. As with English irregular verbs, the vowel changes of the German strong verbs have to be memorized.

- In the table below, the infinitive, past tense, and past participle each have a different stem vowel. Strong verbs often change their stem vowel in the second and third person singular of the present tense too. Therefore, third person present forms also have been given.

Infinitive	Present Tense (3rd person)	Past Tense (3rd person)	Past Participle	Meaning
1. STEM VOWELS *E(I, IE)-A-O*				
befehlen	*befiehlt*	*befahl*	*befohlen*	to order
brechen	*bricht*	*brach*	*gebrochen*	to break
empfehlen	*empfiehlt*	*empfahl*	*empfohlen*	to recommend
nehmen	*nimmt*	*nahm*	*genommen*	to take
sprechen	*spricht*	*sprach*	*gesprochen*	to speak
stehlen	*stiehlt*	*stahl*	*gestohlen*	to steal
sterben	*stirbt*	*starb*	*gestorben*	to die
treffen	*trifft*	*traf*	*getroffen*	to meet
werben	*wirft*	*warb*	*geworben*	to advertise
2. STEM VOWELS *I-A-E*				
bitten	*bittet*	*bat*	*gebeten*	to ask
liegen	*liegt*	*lag*	*gelegen*	to lie
sitzen	*sitzt*	*saß*	*gesessen*	to sit
3. STEM VOWELS *I-A-O*				
beginnen	*beginnt*	*begann*	*begonnen*	to begin
gewinnen	*gewinnt*	*gewann*	*gewonnen*	to win
schwimmen	*schwimmt*	*schwamm*	*geschwommen*	*to swim*

Infinitive	Present Tense (3rd person)	Past Tense (3rd person)	Past Participle	Meaning
4. STEM VOWELS *I-A-U*				
binden	bindet	band	gebunden	to bind
gelingen	gelingt	gelang	gelungen	to succeed
klingen	klingt	klang	geklungen	to sound
schwingen	schwingt	schwang	geschwungen	to swing
singen	singt	sang	gesungen	to sing
springen	springt	sprang	gesprungen	to spring
trinken	trinkt	trank	getrunken	to drink
zwingen	zwingt	zwang	gezwungen	to force

- In the table below, the past participle has the same stem vowel as the infinitive.

Infinitive	Present Tense (3rd person)	Past Tense (3rd person)	Past Participle	Meaning
1. STEM VOWELS *A(Ä)- I(IE)-A*				
fangen	fängt	fing	gefangen	to catch
blasen	bläst	blies	geblasen	to blow
braten	brät	briet	gebraten	to broil
fallen	fällt	fiel	gefallen	to fall
raten	rät	riet	geraten	to advise
schlafen	schläft	schlief	geschlafen	to sleep
2. STEM VOWELS *A(Ä)-U-A*				
backen	bäckt	buk, backte	gebacken	to bake
fahren	fährt	fuhr	gefahren	to drive
graben	gräbt	grub	gegraben	to dig
laden	lädt	lud	geladen	to load
schlagen	schlägt	schlug	geschlagen	to beat
tragen	trägt	trug	getragen	to carry
waschen	wäscht	wusch	gewaschen	to wash

Infinitive	Present Tense (3rd person)	Past Tense (3rd person)	Past Participle	Meaning

3. STEM VOWELS *AU(ÄU)-IE-AU*

Infinitive	Present Tense (3rd person)	Past Tense (3rd person)	Past Participle	Meaning
laufen	*läuft*	*lief*	*gelaufen*	to run

4. STEM VOWELS *E(I, IE)-A-E*

Infinitive	Present Tense (3rd person)	Past Tense (3rd person)	Past Participle	Meaning
essen	*ißt*	*aß*	*gegessen*	to eat
geschehen	*geschieht*	*geschah*	*geschehen*	to happen
lesen	*liest*	*las*	*gelesen*	to read
messen	*mißt*	*maß*	*gemessen*	to measure
sehen	*sieht*	*sah*	*gesehen*	to see
treten	*tritt*	*trat*	*getreten*	to step

5. STEM VOWELS *EI-IE-EI*

Infinitive	Present Tense (3rd person)	Past Tense (3rd person)	Past Participle	Meaning
heißen	*heißt*	*hieß*	*geheißen*	to be called

6. STEM VOWELS *O-A-O*

Infinitive	Present Tense (3rd person)	Past Tense (3rd person)	Past Participle	Meaning
kommen	*kommt*	*kam*	*gekommen*	to come

7. STEM VOWELS *O(Ö)-IE-O*

Infinitive	Present Tense (3rd person)	Past Tense (3rd person)	Past Participle	Meaning
stoßen	*stößt*	*stieß*	*gestoßen*	to push

8. STEM VOWELS *U-IE-U*

Infinitive	Present Tense (3rd person)	Past Tense (3rd person)	Past Participle	Meaning
rufen	*ruft*	*rief*	*gerufen*	to call

- In the table below, the past participle has the same stem vowel as the past tense.

Infinitive	Present Tense (3rd person)	Past Tense (3rd person)	Past Participle	Meaning

1. STEM VOWELS *E-A-A*

Infinitive	Present Tense (3rd person)	Past Tense (3rd person)	Past Participle	Meaning
stehen	*steht*	*stand*	*gestanden*	to stand

Infinitive	Present Tense (3rd person)	Past Tense (3rd person)	Past Participle	Meaning
2. STEM VOWELS *E(I)-O-O*				
heben	*hebt*	*hob*	*gehoben*	to lift
schwellen	*schwillt*	*schwoll*	*geschwollen*	to swell
3. STEM VOWELS *EI-I(I, IE)-I(IE)*				
beißen	*beißt*	*biß*	*gebissen*	to bite
gleichen	*gleicht*	*glich*	*geglichen*	to resemble
reiten	*reitet*	*ritt*	*geritten*	to ride
bleiben	*bleibt*	*blieb*	*geblieben*	to remain
preisen	*preist*	*pries*	*gepriesen*	to praise
schneiden	*schneidet*	*schnitt*	*geschnitten*	to cut
4. STEM VOWELS *IE-O-O*				
bieten	*bietet*	*bot*	*geboten*	to offer
fliegen	*fliegt*	*flog*	*geflogen*	to fly
fließen	*fließt*	*floß*	*geflossen*	to flow
frieren	*friert*	*fror*	*gefroren*	to freeze
ziehen	*zieht*	*zog*	*gezogen*	to draw
5. STEM VOWELS *Ö-O-O*				
schwören	*schwört*	*schwor*	*geschworen*	to swear
6. STEM VOWELS *Ü-O-O*				
lügen	*lügt*	*log*	*gelogen*	to lie

- In the examples below, the first German sentence uses the past tense of the verb, and the second sentence uses the present perfect.

  EXAMPLES:
  Er sprach mit ihr. Er hat mit ihr gesprochen. / He talked with her
  Traf er ihn? Hat er ihn getroffen? / Did he meet him?
  Sie bat ihn um Geld. Sie hat ihn um Geld gebeten. / She asked him for money.
  Gestern begannen wir damit. Gestern haben wir damit begonnen. / Yesterday we started with it.

Sie sang das Lied. Sie hat das Lied gesungen. / She sang the song.

Wir tranken Wein. Wir haben Wein getrunken. / We drank wine.

Das Kind schlief gut. Das Kind hat gut geschlafen. / The child slept well.

Wir aßen viel. Wir haben viel gegessen. / We ate a lot.

Er trug einen Hut. Er hat einen Hut getragen. / He wore a hat.

Sie wusch sich. Sie hat sich gewaschen. / She washed herself.

Du lasest die Zeitung. Du hast die Zeitung gelesen. / You read the paper.

Sahst du sie nicht? Hast du sie nicht gesehen? / Did you not see her?

Transitive and Intransitive Verbs

A *transitive verb* is capable of taking a direct object in the accusative:

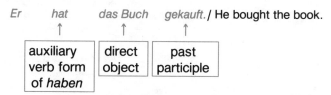

An *intransitive verb* is incapable of taking a direct object:

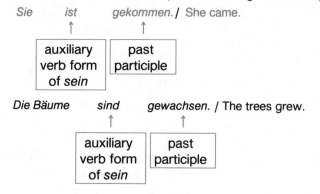

Many German verbs use the auxiliary verb *sein* (instead of *haben*) to form the present perfect *provided that* the main verb is intransitive.

- The following is a list of the more common German verbs that take *sein* as their auxiliary because they denote a change of location:

fahren / to travel	*klettern* / to climb
fallen / to fall	*kommen* / to come
fliegen / to fly	*schwimmen* / to swim
gehen / to go	

- These verbs take *sein* because they indicate a change in condition:

aufwachen / to wake up	*sterben* / to die
einschlafen / to fall asleep	*wachsen* / to grow
ertrinken / to drown	*werden* / to become

- These verbs also take *sein* as their auxiliary:

begegnen / to meet	*gelingen* / to succeed
bleiben / to remain	*mißglücken* / to fail
sein / to be	

Examples of Intransitive Verbs in the Present Perfect

Er ist ins Theater gegangen. / He went to the theater.
Wir sind nach Wien geflogen. / We flew to Vienna.
Sie ist verschwunden. / She disappeared.
Er ist ertrunken. / He drowned.
Ist sie gestorben? / Did she die?
Wir sind zu Hause geblieben. / We stayed at home.
Es ist ihm gelungen. / He succeeded.

Irregular Verbs (see Sec. 8.2 – 2)

Infinitive	Meaning	Past Tense (3rd Person)	Past Participle	Meaning
brennen	to burn	*brannte*	*gebrannt*	burned
kennen	to know	*kannte*	*gekannt*	knew
nennen	to name	*nannte*	*genannt*	named
rennen	to run	*rannte*	*gerannt*	ran
senden	to send	*sandte*	*gesandt*	sent
wenden	to turn	*wandte*	*gewandt*	turned
bringen	to bring	*brachte*	*gebracht*	brought
denken	to think	*dachte*	*gedacht*	thought
wissen	to know	*wußte*	*gewußt*	knew

Note: The forms *sendete, gesendet* (sent), and *wendete, gewendet* (turned) are also used.

EXAMPLES:

Das Haus hat gebrannt. / The house burned.
Er hat mir ein Buch gesandt. / He sent me a book.
Hast du dich an sie gewandt? / Did you turn to her?
Ich habe nicht daran gedacht. / I did not think of it.

§8.2 – 4 Past Perfect Tense

The *past perfect* (or pluperfect) consists of the past tense of the auxiliary verbs *haben* or *sein* plus the past participle of the main verb. This tense indicates a past event that took place *before* another past event.

EXAMPLES:

Er war müde, weil er schlecht geschlafen hatte. / He was tired
because he
had slept

| past | | past perfect | badly. |
| tense | | tense | |

Eva war traurig, weil ihr Freund sie nicht besucht hatte. / Eva
was sad because her friend had not visited her.
Er war zornig, weil sie nicht gekommen war. / He was angry
because she had not come.

Auxiliary Verbs

sein / to be
ich war gewesen / I had been   *wir waren gewesen /* we had
been

du warst gewesen / you had   *ihr wart gewesen /* you had
been   been
er war gewesen / he had   *sie waren gewesen /* they
been   had been

haben / to have
ich hatte gehabt / I had had   *wir hatten gehabt /* we had
had

du hattest gehabt / you had   *ihr hattet gehabt /* you had
had   had
er hatte gehabt / he had had   *sie hatten gehabt /* they had
had

werden / to become
ich war geworden / I had   *wir waren geworden /* we
become   had become
du warst geworden / you   *ihr wart geworden /* you had
had become   become
er war geworden / he had   *sie waren geworden /* they
become   had become

EXAMPLES:

Ich war zu Hause gewesen, als du kamst. / I had been at home
when you came.
Ich hatte Durst gehabt, bevor ich etwas bestellte. / I had been
thirsty before I ordered something.
Sie war Krankenpflegerin geworden, bevor sie Ärztin wurde. /
She had been a nurse before she became a doctor.

8.2–5
Future Tense

The *future* tense is formed from the present tense of the
auxiliary verb *werden* plus the infinitive of the main verb. In
simple sentences, the infinitive usually stands at the end of
the sentence.

EXAMPLES:

Ich werde nach New York fahren. / I will drive to New York.
Wirst du das Buch kaufen? / Will you buy the book?
Wir werden spät aufstehen. / We will get up late.

- Wherever a time phrase (e.g., *nächstes Jahr* / next year, *morgen* / tomorrow) implies that something will happen in the future, the future tense can be replaced by the presen tense:

    Nächstes Jahr fahre ich nach Kanada. / Next year I'll go to Canada.
    Morgen bleibe ich zu Hause. / Tomorrow I'll stay at home.

- In many phrases the present is preferred to the future tense:

    Ich fahr dich zum Bahnhof. / I'll drive you to the station.
    Ich bin gleich dort. / I'll be there right away.
    Wir treffen uns im Café. / We'll meet in the café.

- Sometimes the future tense is used to express probability or likelihood:

    Wo ist Otto? / Where is Otto?
    Er wird in der Schule sein. / He is probably at school.
    Ich habe den neuen Mercedes gesehen, aber der wird zu teue sein. / I have seen the new Mercedes, but it is probably too expensive.

Auxiliary Verbs

sein / to be	
ich werde sein / I will be	*wir werden sein* / we will be
du wirst sein / you will be	*ihr werdet sein* / you will be
er wird sein / he will be	*sie werden sein* / they will be
haben / to have	
ich werde haben / I will have	*wir werden haben* / we will have
du wirst haben / you will have	*ihr werdet haben* / you will have
er wird haben / he will have	*sie werden haben* / they will have

---

werden / to become

ich werde werden / I will become	*wir werden werden* / we will become
du wirst werden / you will become	*ihr werdet werden* / you will become
er wird werden / he will become	*sie werden werden* / they will become

---

EXAMPLES:

Wenn ich komme, wird auch er dort sein./ When I come, he will be there too.

Werden Sie es haben, wenn ich es brauche?/ Will you have it when I need it?

Wird er der nächste Präsident werden?/ Will he become the next president?

§8.2–6 Future Perfect Tense

The *future perfect tense* is formed from the present tense of *werden,* the past participle of the main verb, and the auxiliary verbs *haben* or *sein* at the end of the sentence. This tense is used rarely.

EXAMPLES:

Er wird lange gearbeitet haben./ He will have worked long.

Sie wird sehr müde gewesen sein./ She will have been very tired.

§8.3 THE IMPERATIVE

The *imperative* is used to express requests or commands. In German, an exclamation point is used after a command most of the time. The imperative is used only in the present tense.

- The familiar command in the singular is formed by removing the *-st* or *-t* ending from the second person singular.

EXAMPLES:

Du sagst/ You say.	*Sag!*/ Say!
Du gehst/ You go.	*Geh!*/ Go!
Du trinkst/ You drink.	*Trink!*/ Drink!
Du gibst/ You give.	*Gib!*/ Give!
Du liest/ You read.	*Lies!*/ Read!
Du ißt/ You eat.	*Iß!*/ Eat!

- Verbs that use the umlaut in the second person singular *do not* change the stem vowel in the familiar imperative:

EXAMPLES:

Du wäschst dich./ You wash yourself.	*Wasch dich!*/ Wash yourself.
Du fällst nicht./ You don't fall.	*Fall nicht!*/ Don't fall.

- An *e* should be added to the stem of the verb if the verb ends in *-d, -t, -m, -n,* or *-ig:*

  EXAMPLES:

  Wende dich um! / Turn around.
  Arbeite mehr! / Work more.
  Atme tief! / Breathe deeply.
  Rechne mir das aus! / Figure that out for me.
  Entschuldige, bitte! / Excuse me, please.

- If the infinitive of the verb ends in *-eln,* the *-e-* is eliminated, but an *-e* ending is added:

  EXAMPLES:

Infinitive	*Imperative*
lächeln / to smile	*Lächle!* / Smile!
behandeln / to treat	*Behandle (ihn)!* / Treat (him).

- The familiar command in the plural is formed by using the second person plural without the *ihr:*

  EXAMPLES:

  Kommt nach Hause! / Come home (you two).
  Holt die Zeitung! / Get the paper (boys).
  Kauft nicht zu viel! / Don't buy too much (folks).

- The formal command has the same form for both singular and plural; it is formed by the infinitive followed by *Sie:*

  EXAMPLES:

  Kommen Sie her! / Come here.
  Nehmen Sie Platz! / Take a seat.
  Parken Sie den Wagen! / Park the car.

- The equivalent of the English *"let's . . ."* is formed by using the first person plural of the verb, followed by *wir:*

  EXAMPLES:

  Gehen wir nach Hause! / Let's go home.
  Besuchen wir ihn! / Let's visit him.
  Studieren wir jetzt! / Let's study now.

- The equivalent of the English *"Be so good . . ."* is formed by using *sei* for the singular familiar, *seid* for the plural familiar, and *seien Sie* for the plural formal:

  EXAMPLES:

  Sei so gut und hilf mir damit. / Be so good as to help me with it.
  Seid so gut und helft uns. / Be so good as to help us.
  Seien Sie so gut und helfen Sie uns. / Be so good as to help us.

- The infinitive as command form is used with impersonal instructions and, sometimes, with commands meant to be harsh:

EXAMPLES:

Links fahren. / Drive left.
Einsteigen. / All aboard!
Auf die Bremse steigen. / Step on the brakes.
Mund (Maul) halten. / Shut up!

Note: an exclamation point after commands of this kind is unnecessary.

● Negative commands are formed in the same manner as positive commands. In German there is no construction exactly matching the English *Do not. . . .* or *Don't. . . .*

EXAMPLES:

Sprich nicht so schnell! / Don't talk so fast.
Trinkt nicht so viel Kaffee! / Don't drink so much coffee.
Rauchen Sie nicht! / Don't smoke.
Bitte nicht stören / Please do not disturb.

§8.4 THE SUBJUNCTIVE MOOD

The *subjunctive mood* expresses a point of view, doubt, fear, hope — in short, anything that is not a fact. It can be considered as a counterpart to the indicative mood.

Auxiliary Verbs

The auxiliary verbs *sein* and *haben* in the subjunctive are as follows:

SEIN / TO BE	
Past Tense Indicative	**Present Tense Subjunctive**
ich war / I was	*ich wäre* / I would be
du warst / you were	*du wärest* / you would be
er war / he was	*er wäre* / he would be
wir waren / we were	*wir wären* / we would be
ihr wart / you were	*ihr wäret* / you would be
sie waren / they were	*sie wären* / they would be
Past Tense Subjunctive	
ich wäre gewesen / I would have been	
du wärest gewesen / you would have been	
er wäre gewesen / he would have been	
wir wären gewesen / we would have been	
ihr wäret gewesen / you would have been	
sie wären gewesen / they would have been	

HABEN / TO HAVE	
Past Tense Indicative	**Present Tense Subjunctive**
ich hatte / I had	*ich hätte* / I would have
du hattest / you had	*du hättest* / you would have
er hatte / he had	*er hätte* / he would have
wir hatten / we had	*wir hätten* / we would have
ihr hattet / you had	*ihr hättet* / you would have
sie hatten / they had	*sie hätten* / they would have

Past Tense Subjunctive

ich hätte gehabt / I would have had
du hättest gehabt / you would have had
er hätte gehabt / he would have had
wir hätten gehabt / we would have had
ihr hättet gehabt / you would have had
sie hätten gehabt / they would have had

EXAMPLES:
Wäre ich nur jünger!

OR

Wenn ich nur jünger wäre! / If only I were younger!
Wärest du nur hier gewesen!

OR

Wenn du nur hier gewesen wärest! / If only you had been here
Hätte er nur mehr Geduld!

OR

Wenn er nur mehr Geduld hätte! / If only he had more patience
Hätten wir nur mehr Geld gehabt!

OR

Wenn wir nur mehr Geld gehabt hätten! / If only we had had
  more money!

• Here are some other verbs used with *wäre* and *hätte:*

Wärest du nur gekommen! / If only you had come!
Hätten Sie es nur getan! / If only you had done it!

Weak Verbs

The present tense of the subjunctive for weak verbs is
identical to the past tense indicative.

ich glaubte / I believed	*wir glaubten* / we believed
du glaubtest / you believed	*ihr glaubtet* / you believed
er glaubte / he believed	*sie glaubten* / they believed

EXAMPLE:
Glaubte er mir nur!

OR

Wenn er mir nur glaubte! / If he would only believe me!

- For clarity's sake, particularly in the spoken and colloquial use of the language, the form *würde* (would) is used to express weak verbs (and many strong ones) in the subjunctive.

Forms of *würde*	
ich würde / I would	*wir würden* / we would
du würdest / you would	*ihr würdet* / you would
er würde / he would	*sie würden* / they would

EXAMPLES:
Würde er mir nur glauben! / If only he would believe me!
Würdest du das Haus kaufen? / Would you buy the house?
Sie weiß, daß ich es sagen würde. / She knows that I would say it.
Sie weiß, daß ich es gesagt haben würde. / She knows that I would have said it.

Strong and Irregular Verbs

Strong and irregular verbs are formed by adding the subjunctive endings -*e*, -*est*, -*e*, -*en*, -*et*, and -*en* to the stem of the verb in the past tense. Verbs containing the vowels *a*, *o*, or *u* in the stem add an umlaut.

Infinitive	Past Tense	Present Tense Subjunctive
schlafen / to sleep	*ich schlief* / I slept	*ich schliefe* / I would sleep
geben / to give	*du gabst* / you gave	*du gäbest* / you would give
fliegen / to fly	*er flog* / he flew	*er flöge* / he would fly
schlagen / to beat	*wir schlugen* / we beat	*wir schlügen* / we would beat
bringen / to bring	*ihr brachtet* / you brought	*ihr brächtet* / you would bring
wissen / to know	*sie wußten* / they knew	*sie wüßten* / they would know

EXAMPLES:
Mit einer Million auf der Bank, schliefe ich besser, schlüge mir die Sorgen aus dem Kopf, und flöge morgen nach Tahiti. / With a million in the bank, I would sleep better, forget my troubles, and fly to Tahiti tomorrow.
Er brächte dir gern Blumen. / He would like to bring you flowers.
Wüßten wir nur die Antwort! / If only we knew the answer.

Some strong and irregular verbs in the subjunctive, present and past tense, 1st person singular, are shown in the table

Infinitive	Past Tense Indicative	Present Tense Subjunctive	Past Tense Subjunctive
bleiben	ich blieb / I stayed	ich bliebe / I would stay	ich wäre geblieben / I would have stayed
bringen	ich brachte / I brought	ich brächte / I would bring	ich hätte gebracht / I would have brought
denken	ich dachte / I thought	ich dächte / I would think	ich hätte gedacht / I would have thought
finden	ich fand / I found	ich fände / I would find	ich hätte gefunden / I would have found
gehen	ich ging / I went	ich ginge / I would go	ich wäre gegangen / I would have gone
halten	ich hielt / I held	ich hielte / I would hold	ich hätte gehalten / I would have held
kommen	ich kam / I came	ich käme / I would come	ich wäre gekommen / I would have come
wissen	ich wußte / I knew	ich wüßte / I would know	ich hätte gewußt / I would have known

EXAMPLES:

Present Tense Subjunctive
Ich wollte, er bliebe zu Hause.

OR

Ich wollte, er würde zu Hause bleiben. / I wished he would stay home.

Past Tense Subjunctive
Ich wollte, er wäre zu Hause geblieben. / I wished he would have stayed home.

Present Tense Subjunctive
Ich wünschte, er fände den Ring.

OR

Ich wünschte, er würde den Ring finden. / I wished he would find the ring.

Past Tense Subjunctive
Ich wünschte, er hätte den Ring gefunden. / I wished he would have found the ring.

Present Tense Subjunctive
Ich wollte, er wüßte die Adresse.

OR

Ich wollte, er würde die Adresse wissen. / I wished he would know the address.

Past Tense Subjunctive
Ich wollte, er hätte die Adresse gewußt. / I wished he would have known the address.

Special Subjunctive

The subjunctive endings -e, -est, -e, -en, -et, and -en can also be added to the infinitive stem (the infinitive without -en) to form a "Special Subjunctive" (also called "Present Subjunctive I" or "Present Subjunctive Primary"). These forms, sometimes translated by "may" or "let," are primarily literary but are often used in news reports when writers and broadcasters quote indirectly from others.

EXAMPLES:

Es lebe die Königin (die Republik, der Wein)!/ Long live the queen (the republic, wine)!

Sie komme! Sie töte mich!(Schiller's *Maria Stuart*) / Let her come! Let her kill me!

Der Präsident sagt, er könne es nicht tun./ The president says he can't do it.

§8.5 THE CONDITIONAL MOOD

The *conditional mood* is the grammatical form usually introduced by *wenn* (if). It expresses a condition: "I would do it, if . . . ." It is used in the same way as the English conditional.

- The indicative mood must be used in both parts of a conditional sentence if nothing in the clause introduced by *wenn* is contrary to fact.

  EXAMPLES:

  Wenn ich Zeit habe, lese ich ein Buch.

  OR

  Ich lese ein Buch, wenn ich Zeit habe.

  OR

  Habe ich Zeit, so lese ich ein Buch. / If I have time, I will read a book.

  Note: in the last version the *wenn* is implied.

- Present contrary-to-fact situations are expressed by the present tense of the subjunctive.

  EXAMPLES:

  Wenn ich Zeit hätte, würde ich ein Buch lesen. / If I had time, I would read a book.

  Wenn es nicht schneite, würde ich früher kommen.

  OR

  Wenn es nicht schneite, käme ich früher. / If it did not snow, I would come earlier.

- Past contrary-to-fact situations can be expressed by the past tense of the subjunctive or by the *würde* construction:

Subjunctive:
Wenn es nicht geschneit hätte, wäre ich früher nach Hause gekommen.
Wurde Construction:
Wenn es nicht geschneit hätte, würde ich früher nach Hause gekommen sein. / If it had not snowed, I would have come home earlier.

- Some of the umlauted subjunctive verbs are often replaced by the *würde* construction: *ich brächte, ich würde bringen* (I would bring); *ich dächte, ich würde denken* (I would think); *ich fände, ich würde finden* (I would find); *ich käme, ich würde kommen* (I would come).

- Sometimes the *würde* in a *wenn* clause can be substituted for a modal verb (see §8.8), although the meaning of the sentence might change slightly.

  Wenn du es mir bringen solltest (instead of *bringen würdest* or *brächtest*), *würde ich mich sehr freuen.* / If you would bring it to me, I would be very happy.

  Wenn er mir helfen wollte (instead of *hülfe* or *helfen würde*), *könnte ich studieren.* / If he would (wanted to) help me, I could study.

  Wenn ich mit ihm sprechen könnte (instead of *spräche* or *sprechen würde*), *wäre die Sache in Ordnung.* / If I could talk to him, the situation would be all right.

- Constructions introduced by *als ob* (as if):

  Er schreit, als ob er verrückt wäre. / He shouts as if he were crazy.
  Es sieht aus, als ob es morgen schneien würde. / It looks as if it would snow tomorrow.
  Er tut, als ob er das nicht gewußt hätte. / He acts as if he had not known that.

§8.6
MISCELLANEOUS
CATEGORIES

§8.6 – 1
Impersonal
Verbs

Impersonal verbs, introduced by the pronoun *es* (it), are even more common in German than in English.

- Impersonal verbs referring to natural phenomena are often used in both languages.

  EXAMPLES:
  Es ist warm. / It is warm.   *Es regnet.* / It rains
  Es ist kalt. / It is cold.   (is raining).

Es schneit. / It snows
(is snowing).
Es friert. / It is freezing.
Es tagt. / It dawns
(is dawning).
Es dämmert. / It darkens
(is getting dark).

Es ist schwül. / It is muggy.
Es donnert. / It's thundering.
(There's thunder.)
Es blitzt. / There is lightning.

- Here are some expressions that have as subject the impersonal pronoun *es* in German but are usually translated by a personal pronoun (I, you, he, etc.) in English.

> *Es enttäuscht mich (sie, uns), daß . . . /* I am (she is, we are)
>   disappointed (it disappoints me, her, us) that . . .
> *Es erstaunt mich, daß . . . /* I am amazed (it amazes me)
>   that . . .
> *Es freut mich, daß . . . /* I am glad (it gladdens me) that . . .
> *Es gefällt mir hier. /* I like it here.
> *Es tut mir leid. /* I am sorry.
> *Es ist mir recht. /* I agree to it.

- Here are some examples using the expression *es gibt* (there is, there are)

> *Es gibt heute Wiener Schnitzel. /* There is (we have) Wiener
>   Schnitzel (veal cutlet) today.
> *Es gibt nichts zu tun hier. /* There is nothing to do here.
> *Es gibt einen Brief für dich. /* There is a letter for you.
> *Was gibt es heute zum Abendessen? /* What is there for
>   dinner tonight?
> *So etwas gibt es nicht. /* There is no such thing.
> *Das gab es nicht. /* That did not exist.

8.6–2
Verbs Taking the Dative

The following is a partial list of verbs that take the dative (indirect object) in German but the accusative (the direct object) in English.

antworten / to answer	*Antworte mir! /* Answer me.
begegnen / to meet	*Wir sind ihm begegnet. /* We met him.
danken / to thank	*Ich danke dir. /* I thank you.
dienen / to serve	*Er diente ihm. /* He served him.

drohen / to threaten	*Drohen Sie mir nicht!* / Don't threaten me.
entgehen / to evade	*Er entging der Strafe.* / He evaded punishment.
folgen / follow	*Sie folgte mir.* / She followed me.
gehorchen / to obey	*Das Kind gehorcht mir.* / The child obeys me.
glauben / to believe	*Meine Frau glaubt mir.* / My wife believes me.
gratulieren / to congratulate	*Ich gratuliere Ihnen.* / I congratulate you.
helfen / to help	*Wir helfen ihr.* / We help her.
imponieren / to impress	*Er imponiert mir.* / He impresses me.
passen / to fit, suit	*Das paßt mir gut.* / That suits me fine.
schaden / to hurt	*Wird mir das schaden?* / Will that hurt me?
schmeicheln / to flatter	*Schmeicheln Sie mir nicht!* / Don't flatter me.
vertrauen / to trust	*Vertrauen Sie mir!* / Trust me.
verzeihen / to forgive	*Verzeihen Sie mir!* / Forgive me.

§8.6–3 Reflexive Verbs

Reflexive verbs usually relate an action that is directed back to the subject. The reflexive verb *rasieren* (to shave oneself) is conjugated below (present tense).

ich rasiere mich / I shave (myself)	*wir rasieren uns* / we shave (ourselves)
du rasierst dich / you shave (yourself)	*ihr rasiert euch* / you shave (yourselves)
er rasiert sich / he shaves (himself)	*sie rasieren sich* / they shave (themselves)

- Reflexive verbs usually take the accusative form of the reflexive pronoun (*mich, dich, sich;* see §7.1–3).
- Some common reflexive verbs are listed in the table below.

Infinitive	Third Person Singular
sich beeilen / to hurry	*Er beeilt sich.* / He hurries.
sich erholen / to recover (from)	*Sie erholt sich (davon).* / She recovers (from it).
sich erinnern / to remember	*Sie erinnert sich (daran).* / She remembers (it).

Infinitive	Third Person Singular
sich erkälten / to catch a cold	*Sie erkältet sich.* / She catches a cold.
sich fragen / to wonder	*Er fragt sich (darüber).* / He wonders (about it).
sich freuen / to be glad	*Sie freut sich (darüber).* / She is glad (about it).
sich fürchten / to fear	*Er fürchtet sich (davor).* / He is afraid (of it).
sich gewöhnen / to get used to	*Er gewöhnt sich (daran).* / He gets used (to it).
sich irren / to be mistaken	*Sie irrt sich.* / She is mistaken.
sich lohnen / to be worthwhile.	*Lohnt sich das?* / Is that worthwhile?
sich sehnen / to long (for).	*Er sehnt sich (nach jemand[em]).* / He longs (for someone).
sich setzen / to sit (down).	*Er setzt sich.* / He sits down.
sich verirren / to get lost.	*Er verirrt sich.* / He gets lost.
sich wundern / to be surprised	*Sie wundert sich (darüber).* / She is surprised (about it).

EXAMPLES:

Beeile dich! Es ist spät. / Hurry up. It is late.

Er erinnert sich an ihren Geburtstag. / He remembers her birthday.

Geben Sie acht, daß Sie sich nicht erkälten. / Be careful that you don't catch cold.

Setzen Sie sich, bitte! / Sit down, please.

Wir haben uns in den Bergen verirrt. / We lost our way in the mountains.

Ich wundere mich über seine Dummheit. / I am surprised at his stupidity.

Ich frage mich, ob sich das lohnt. / I wonder if that's worthwhile.

- Reflexive verbs taking the dative reflexive pronoun

  EXAMPLES

  Ich kaufe mir einen Wagen. / I buy (myself) a car.
  Du kaufst dir einen Wagen. / You buy (yourself) a car.
  Er kauft sich einen Wagen. / He buys (himself) a car.
  Wir kaufen uns einen Wagen. / We buy (ourselves) a car.
  Ihr kauft euch einen Wagen. / You buy (yourselves) a car.
  Sie kaufen sich einen Wagen. / They buy (themselves) a car.

Infinitive	Example
sich etwas holen	*Hol mir die Zeitung!* / Get the paper.
sich Sorgen machen	*Mach dir keine Sorgen!* / Don't worry.
sich etwas verbitten	*Das verbitte ich mir.* / I won't stand for that.
sich etwas vergönnen	*Heute vergönne ich mir das.* / Today I'll treat myself to this.
sich wehtun	*Ich habe mir wehgetan.* / I hurt myself.
sich den Hut aufsetzen	*Er setzt sich den Hut auf.* / He puts on his hat.

Infinitive	Example
sich die Zähne putzen	*Er putzt sich die Zähne.* / He brushes his teeth.
sich das Haar waschen	*Er wäscht sich das Haar.* / He washes his hair.

Note: in reference to articles of clothing and parts of the body, the German differs from the English (see the last three sentences in the table above).

§8.6–4 Separable Prefixes

Separable prefixes can stand alone as words in their own right. They are usually removed from the verb in the present and the past tense and put at the end of the sentence.

The following table contains some of the more common verbs with separable prefixes.

Separable Prefix	Infinitive	Example
ab / off	*abnehmen* / to take off	*Er nimmt den Hut ab.* / He takes off the hat.
an / at, on	*anfangen* / to begin	*Fangen Sie an!* / Begin.
auf / up	*aufmachen* / to open	*Machen Sie die Tür auf!* / Open the door.
aus / out	*ausgehen* / to go out	*Wir gehen aus.* / We go out.
bei / by, with, at	*beitragen* / to contribute	*Er trägt dazu bei.* / He contributes to it.
ein / in, into	*einladen* / to invite	*Sie laden uns ein.* / They invite us.
fort / away	*fortgehen* / to go away	*Gehen wir fort!* / Let's go away.
heim / home	*heimkehren* / to return	*Sie kehrte heim.* / She returned home.
herein / in, into	*hereinkommen* / to come in	*Kommen Sie herein!* / Come in.
hinunter / down	*hinuntergehen* / to go down	*Gehen Sie hinunter.* / Go down.
mit / with	*mitnehmen* / to take along	*Sie nahm es mit.* / She took it along.
nach / after	*nachdenken* / to think about	*Ich werde darüber nachdenken.* / I'll think about it.
nieder / down	*niederfallen* / to fall down	*Er fiel nieder.* / He fell down.
vor / before	*vorhaben* / to have in mind	*Was hast du vor?* / What do you have in mind?
weg / away	*wegnehmen* / to take away	*Er nahm es weg.* / He took it away.
zu / to	*zugeben* / to admit	*Sie gab es zu.* / She admitted it.
zurück / back	*zurückfahren* / to drive back	*Er fuhr zurück.* / He drove back.

- In tenses other than the present and the past, the verb and the prefix are not separated. In the present perfect, past perfect, and future perfect, -*ge*- is inserted between the prefix and the verb. In a dependent clause there is no separation either.

  Future Tense
  Ich werde heute ausgehen. / I will go out today.
  Present Perfect, Past Perfect
  Sie haben uns eingeladen. / They invited us.
  Er war heimgekehrt. / He had returned.
  Dependent Clause
  Sie war dort, als er niederfiel. / She was there when he fell down.

8.6–5
Inseparable Prefixes

The prefixes *be-*, *emp-*, *ent-*, *er-*, *ver-*, and *zer-* are inseparable from their verbs. The past participle *does not* take the
prefix *ge-*. Inseparable prefixes are never stressed.

Here are some of the more common verbs with inseparable prefixes.

behalten / to keep	*Er hat sein Geld behalten.* / He kept his money.
bekommen / to get	*Er wird es bekommen.* / He will get it.
empfangen / to receive	*Sie empfing ein gutes Gehalt.* / She received a good salary.
empfehlen / to recommend	*Ich kann ihn bestens empfeh-len.* / I can recommend him very highly.
entdecken / to discover	*Wer hat Amerika entdeckt?* / Who discovered America?
erreichen / to achieve	*Er hat es erreicht.* / He achieved it.
verkaufen / to sell	*Wir haben es verkauft.* / We sold it.
vermieten / to rent	*Er hat es ihm vermietet.* / He rented it to him.
verstehen / to understand	*Er hat mich verstanden.* / He understood me.
versagen / to fail	*Hat er versagt?* / Did he fail?
zerstören / to destroy	*Der Krieg zerstörte alles.* / The war destroyed everything.

8.7
PRESENT PARTICIPLES AND VERBAL NOUNS

The *present participle* is formed by adding *-d* to the
infinitive.

Infinitive:*singen* / to sing
Present Participle:*singend* / singing

Note: There are two exceptions:
the present participle of *sein* is *seiend* (being); the
present participle of *tun* is *tuend* (doing).

• When the present participle is used as an adjective, it takes
the same endings as an adjective.

Sie ist ein wandelndes Konversationslexikon./ She is a walking encyclopedia.

Sie kennt die wachsenden Gefahren./ She knows of the growing dangers.

Er betrachtet das schlafende Kind./ He looks at the sleeping child.

Dieses Hotel ist hauptsächlich für Reisende:/ This hotel is mainly for commercial travelers.

- When the present participle is used as an adverb, it has no declension.

Der Film war überraschend gut. / The film was surprisingly good.
Es hat dauernd geschneit. / It has been snowing constantly.

§8.7–1 VERBAL NOUNS

- The present participle is used only as an adjective (or adjectival noun [see §6.1-4], as in *Reisende* above) and as an adverb, not as a verbal noun. The German verbal noun is the capitalized infinitive. It is always neuter.

Laß das Rauchen!/ Stop smoking!
Das Reisen ist ihm keine Freude mehr./ Traveling is no fun for him anymore.
Das Wandern ist gesund./ Hiking is healthy.

§8.8 MODAL VERBS

Modal verbs do not describe an action but an attitude toward it. A modal verb normally is followed by a complementary or "completing" infinitive.

Ich muß gehen./ I must go.
Ich darf gehen./ I may go.

There are six modal verbs in German:

können / to be able to, to be capable of, could
dürfen / to be allowed to, may
müssen / to have to, to be obliged to, must
mögen / to like to, may
sollen / to be supposed to, should
wollen / to want to, to wish to

KÖNNEN / TO BE ABLE TO, TO BE CAPABLE OF, COULD

Present Tense	Past Tense
ich kann / I can	*ich konnte* / I could
du kannst / you can	*du konntest* / you could
er kann / he can	*er konnte* / he could
wir können / we can	*wir konnten* / we could
ihr könnt / you can	*ihr konntet* / you could
sie können / they can	*sie konnten* / they could

EXAMPLES:

Ich kann gut schwimmen. / I can swim well.
Wir können nach Bonn fliegen. / We can fly to Bonn.
Er konnte Deutsch sprechen. / He could speak German.
Du kannst das machen. / You are able to do that.
Das kann nicht passieren. / That cannot happen.
Ihr könnt Bridge spielen. / You can play bridge.
Kann sie zu Hause bleiben? / Can she stay at home?
Kann er das tun? / Is he capable of doing that?
Konnten Sie ihm helfen? / Were you able to help him?
Konnte sie kommen? / Could she come?

DÜRFEN / TO BE ALLOWED TO, MAY

Present Tense	Past Tense
ich darf / I may	*ich durfte* / I was allowed to
du darfst / you may	*du durftest* / you were allowed to
er darf / he may	*er durfte* / he was allowed to
wir dürfen / we may	*wir durften* / we were allowed to
ihr dürft / you may	*ihr durftet* / you were allowed to
sie dürfen / they may	*sie durften* / they were allowed to

EXAMPLES:

Du darfst ins Theater gehen. / You are allowed to (may) go to the theater.
Ihr durftet spielen. / You were allowed to play.
Sie darf Gefrorenes essen. / She may eat ice cream.
Die Kinder dürfen spielen. / The children may play.
Sie durfte nicht ausgehen. / She was not allowed to go out.
Wir durften hier rauchen. / We were allowed to smoke here.
Dürft ihr hierbleiben? / Are you allowed to stay here?
Dürfen wir mitkommen? / May we come along?
Darf ich Sie begleiten? / May I accompany you?
Durftest du ihn sehen? / Were you allowed to see him?

MÜSSEN / TO HAVE TO, TO BE OBLIGED TO, MUST	
Present Tense	**Past Tense**
ich muß / I must	*ich mußte* / I had to
du mußt / you must	*du mußtest* / you had to
er muß / he must	*er mußte* / he had to
wir müssen / we must	*wir mußten* / we had to
ihr müßt / you must	*ihr mußtest* / you had to
sie müssen / they must	*sie mußten* / they had to

EXAMPLES:

Ich muß nach Hause gehen. / I have to (must) go home.
Sie müssen jetzt studieren. / They have to (must) study now.
Mußtest du weggehen? / Did you have to go away?
Er muß jetzt aufstehen. / He has to (must) get up now.
Wir mußten Klavier spielen. / We had to play the piano.
Sie mußte Peter abholen. / She had to pick up Peter.
Mußtet ihr lange warten? / Did you have to wait long?
Was müssen wir noch tun? / What else do we have to do?
Müßt ihr ihm zuhören? / Do you have to listen to him?
Mußt du so viel essen? / Do you have to eat so much?

MÖGEN / TO LIKE, MAY	
Present Tense	**Past Tense**
ich mag / I like	*ich mochte* / I liked
du magst / you like	*du mochtest* / you liked
er mag / he likes	*er mochte* / he liked
wir mögen / we like	*wir mochten* / we liked
ihr mögt / you like	*ihr mochtet* / you liked
sie mögen / they like	*sie mochten* / they liked

EXAMPLES:

Ich mag ihn nicht. / I don't like him.
Er mag 50 Jahre alt sein. / He may (might) be 50 years old.
Wir mochten keinen Kaffee. / We did not like (want) any coffee.
Das mag wohl sein. / That may well be.
Er mochte sie nicht. / He did not like her.
Sie mag das nicht hören. / She doesn't like to hear that.
Magst du Wein oder Bier? / Do you like wine or beer?
Mögt ihr ihn nicht? / Don't you like him?
Mögen Sie klassische Musik? / Do you like classical music?
Mochten Sie nicht das Brot? / Didn't you like the bread?

SOLLEN / TO BE TO, BE SUPPOSED TO, OUGHT TO, SHOULD

Present Tense	Past Tense
ich soll / I am to (I should) *du sollst* / you are to (you should) *er soll* / he is to (he should) *wir sollen* / we are to (we should) *ihr sollt* / you are to (you should) *sie sollen* / they are to (they should)	*ich sollte* / I should (have) *du solltest* / you should (have) *er sollte* / he should (have) *wir sollten* / we should (have) *ihr solltet* / you should (have) *sie sollten* / they should (have)

EXAMPLES:

Er sollte sie besucht haben. / He should have visited her.
Du sollst höflich sein. / You ought to be polite.
Er soll reich sein. / He is supposed to be rich.
Ich sollte ihm schreiben. / I ought to (should) write him.
Ursula soll in Wien sein. / Ursula is supposed to be in Vienna.
Ihr sollt euch schämen! / You should be ashamed of yourselves.
Wann sollen wir dort sein? / When are we supposed to be there?
Soll ich ihn anrufen? / Shall I call him?
Soll er sich entschuldigen? / Is he to apologize?
Sollten wir ihn unterstützen? / Ought we to support him?

WOLLEN / TO WANT TO, TO WISH TO

Present Tense	Past Tense
ich will / I want to *du willst* / you want to *er will* / he wants to *wir wollen* / we want to *ihr wollt* / you want to *sie wollen* / they want to	*ich wollte* / I wanted to *du wolltest* / you wanted to *er wollte* / he wanted to *wir wollten* / we wanted to *ihr wolltet* / you wanted to *sie wollten* / they wanted to

EXAMPLES:

Was wollen Sie heute machen? / What do you want to do today?
Willst du mir helfen? / Do you want to help me?
Wollten Sie hierbleiben? / Did you wish to stay here?
Wir wollen jetzt studieren. / We want to study now.
Sie will das Buch lesen. / She wants to read the book.
Ich will das nicht tun. / I do not wish to do that.
Wollt ihr ins Kino gehen? / Do you want to go to the movies?
Will er nach Berlin fliegen? / Does he want to fly to Berlin?
Wolltest du ihn besuchen? / Did you want to call on him?
Was wollte sie ihm sagen? / What did she want to tell him?

- When they have a complementary infinitive, modal verbs in the future and in the tenses of the perfect use a construction called the "double infinitive." The future of modals is formed by the present tense of *werden*, the infinitive of the complementary verb, plus the infinitive of the modal verb.

    EXAMPLES:
    Ich werde nach Hause gehen müssen. / I will have to go home
    Er wird es nicht schreiben können. / He won't be able to write it
    Sie werden nicht kommen dürfen. / They won't be allowed to come.

- Similarly, the present perfect and past perfect of modal verbs are formed with a form of *haben*, the infinitive of the complementary verb, plus the infinitive of the modal verb.

    EXAMPLES:
    Ich habe nicht schwimmen können. / I have not been able (I was not able) to swim.
    Wir haben das Kind sehen müssen. / We had to see the child.
    Er hatte nicht rauchen dürfen. / He had not been (was not) allowed to smoke.

- The verbs *sehen* (to see), *hören* (to hear), and *helfen* (to help) also take the double infinitive construction.

    EXAMPLES:
    Ich sehe sie kommen. / I see her coming.
    Ich habe sie kommen sehen. / I saw her coming.
    Ich höre ihn sprechen. / I hear him talking.
    Ich habe ihn sprechen hören. / I heard him talking.
    Ich helfe ihm das Radio reparieren. / I help him repair the radio.
    Ich habe ihm das Radio reparieren helfen.

    OR

    Ich habe ihm geholfen, das Radio zu reparieren. / I helped him repair the radio.

- There are two forms for the past participle of modal verbs. One is identical to the infinitive.

    Er hatte nicht rauchen dürfen. / He had not been (was not) allowed to smoke.

- The other, when used in a sentence without a complementary infinitive, is formed with the prefix *ge-*, just like any other verb.

    gekonnt, gedurft, gemußt, gemocht, gesollt, gewollt

- In the examples below, the complementary infinitive is not expressed but is understood: *Er darf es nicht (tun). Wir müssen nach Hause (gehen). Ich mag keinen Spinat (essen). Er soll das nicht (tun). Sie will nach Amerika (fahren).* Therefore, it can be omitted. In the examples with the present perfect tense please note that because the complementary infinitives have been omitted, the *ge-* form of the past participle is used.

  EXAMPLES:

  Er darf es nicht. / He is not allowed to do it.
  Sie durfte es nicht. / She was not allowed to do it.
  Wir müssen nach Hause. / We must (have to) go home.
  Wir haben nach Hause gemußt. / We had to go home.
  Ich mag keinen Spinat. / I don't like (want) spinach.
  Ich habe ihn nicht gemocht. / I did not like him.
  Er soll das nicht. / He should not do it.
  Er hat das nicht gesollt. / He was not supposed to do that.
  Sie will nach Amerika. / She wants to go to America.
  Sie hat nach Amerika gewollt. / She wanted to go to America.

- The use of *können* as a transitive verb meaning "to know" is limited mostly to subjects of learning, such as languages.

  EXAMPLES:

  Ich kann Spanisch. / I know Spanish.
  Er hatte Deutsch gekonnt. / He had known German.

8.9
THE PASSIVE VOICE

8.9–1
Present Tense

In the *active voice* — the form that we have been dealing with up to now — the subject brings about the action represented by the verb. In the *passive voice,* the subject is passive: it is being acted upon.

Active Voice
Karl füttert den Vogel. / Karl feeds the bird.
Passive Voice
Der Vogel wird von Karl gefüttert. / The bird is being fed by Karl.

The agent (Karl) can also be omitted in the passive sentence:

Der Vogel wird gefüttert. / The bird is being fed.

In the passive voice we use a form of the auxiliary verb *werden* and the past participle of the main verb. The direct object in the original sentence *(Vogel)* now becomes the subject. The former subject or agent *(Karl)* becomes the object of the preposition *von (von Karl),* taking the dative.

- If the agent in the passive sentence is a living being, we us*e* *von.* If the agent is the means by which something is done, it becomes the object of the preposition *durch,* taking the accusative. This is especially true in the case of impersonal forces (fire, flood, storm, rain, etc).

  EXAMPLES:
  Active Voice
  Der Sturm entwurzelt die Bäume. / The storm uproots the tree*s*
  Passive Voice
  Die Bäume werden durch den Sturm entwurzelt. / The trees ar*e*
    being uprooted by the storm.
  Active Voice
  Der Mann repariert den Eisschrank. / The man repairs the
    refrigerator.
  Passive Voice
  Der Eisschrank wird von dem Mann repariert. / The refrigerato*r*
    is being repaired by the man.

- Many intransitive verbs that take the dative (indirect object*)* such as *antworten* (to answer), *danken* (to thank), *gehorchen* (to obey), *helfen* (to help), and *verzeihen* (to forgive), can be used in the passive voice (see §8.6–2).

  EXAMPLES:
  Der Lehrer antwortet den Schülern. / The teacher answers the*ir*
    pupils.
  Dem Lehrer wird von den Schülern geantwortet. / The teacher
    is being answered by the pupils.
  Die Mutter verzeiht ihrem Sohn. / The mother forgives her son*.*
  Dem Sohn wird von seiner Mutter verziehen. / The son is bein*g*
    forgiven by his mother.
  Er hilft mir. / He helps me.
  Mir wird von ihm geholfen. / I am being helped by him.

§8.9–2
Past Tense

The past tense is formed from the past tense of *werden (wurde)* plus the past participle of the main verb.

Ich wurde gesehen / I was seen.	*Wir wurden gesehen.* / We were seen.
Du wurdest gesehen. / You were seen.	*Ihr wurdet gesehen.* / You were seen.
Er wurde gesehen. / He was seen.	*Sie wurden gesehen.* / They were seen.

EXAMPLES:
Ich sah meinen Freund. / I saw my friend.
Mein Freund wurde von mir gesehen. / My friend was seen by me.
Bomben zerstörten die Stadt. / Bombs destroyed the city.
Die Stadt wurde durch Bomben zerstört. / The city was
  destroyed by bombs.

§8.9-3 Present Perfect Tense

The present perfect tense is formed from the present tense of *sein,* plus the past participle of the main verb, plus *worden* (not *geworden*).

> *Ich bin besucht worden.* / I have been (was) visited.
> *Du bist besucht worden.* / You have been (were) visited.
> *Er ist besucht worden.* / He has been (was) visited.
> *Wir sind besucht worden.* / We have been (were) visited.
> *Ihr seid besucht worden.* / You have been (were) visited.
> *Sie sind besucht worden.* / They have been (were) visited.

EXAMPLES:

Ich habe Karl besucht. / I (have) visited Karl.
Karl ist von mir besucht worden. / Karl has been (was) visited by me.
Eine Seuche hat das Volk getötet. / An epidemic (has) killed the people.
Das Volk ist durch eine Seuche getötet worden. / The people have been (were) killed by an epidemic.

§8.9-4 Past Perfect Tense

The *past perfect tense* is formed from the past tense of *sein,* plus the past participle of the main verb, plus *worden.*

> *Ich war behandelt worden.* / I had been treated.
> *Du warst behandelt worden.* / You had been treated.
> *Er war behandelt worden.* / He had been treated.
> *Wir waren behandelt worden.* / We had been treated.
> *Ihr wart behandelt worden.* / You had been treated.
> *Sie waren behandelt worden.* / They had been treated.

EXAMPLES:

Dr. Müller hatte mich behandelt. / Dr. Müller had treated me.
Ich war von Dr. Müller behandelt worden. / I had been treated by Dr. Müller.

§8.9-5 Future Tense

The future tense is formed from the present tense of *werden,* plus the past participle of the main verb, plus *werden.*

> *Ich werde gefunden werden.* / I will be found.
> *Du wirst gefunden werden.* / You will be found.
> *Er wird gefunden werden.* / He will be found.
> *Wir werden gefunden werden.* / We will be found.
> *Ihr werdet gefunden werden.* / You will be found.
> *Sie werden gefunden werden.* / They will be found.

EXAMPLES:

Karl wird das Buch finden. / Karl will find the book.
Das Buch wird von Karl gefunden werden. / The book will be found by Karl.

§8.9–6 Modal Auxiliaries

Modal auxiliary verbs (*können, dürfen, müssen, mögen, sollen, wollen* [see §8.8]) have no passive voice, but they can be followed by a passive infinitive (*kann werden, soll werden, muß werden,* etc.).

EXAMPLES:

Das kann getan werden. / That can be done.
Die Rechnungen müssen bezahlt werden. / The bills must be p⟨
Die Ware sollte verkauft worden sein. / The merchandise shoul⟨ have been sold.

§8.9–7 Substitutes for the Passive Voice

The passive voice is used less frequently in German than it is in English. Sentences in the active voice using the word *man* (the impersonal "one") or reflexive verb constructions can be used instead.

EXAMPLES:

Man glaubt, daß . . . / It is believed that . . . (One believes that . . .)
Das tut man hier nicht. / That is not done here. (One does not do that here.)
Wie spricht man das aus? / How is that pronounced?
Man weiß, daß er reich ist. / He is believed to be rich.
Man sah ihn ins Theater gehen. / He was seen entering the the⟨
Das versteht sich von selbst. / That is understood.
Das lernt sich schnell. / That is quickly (to be) learned.
Das sagt sich leicht. / That is easily said.
Das läßt sich arrangieren. / That can be arranged.

§8.9–8 The False Passive

The true passive is always formed with *werden* and the past participle of the main verb; it expresses an ongoing action. The false, or apparent, passive is formed with the verb *sein* and the past participle; it expresses the *result* of an action.

*Die Tür **wird** geschlossen.* / The door is being closed (true passive).
*Die Tür **ist** geschlossen.* / The door is closed (false passive).

In the second sentence the past participle *(geschlossen)* functions as an adjective.

EXAMPLES:

Ongoing Action
*Die Uhr **wird** repariert.* / The watch is being repaired.
Result of an Action
*Die Uhr **ist** repariert.* / The watch is repaired.

§9.

Adverbs

Adverbs are words that modify verbs, adjectives, or other adverbs. They indicate place, time, manner, and intensity.

Er spricht **schnell.**   He talks fast.
Das Mädchen ist **sehr** *hübsch.* / The girl is very pretty.
Sie geht **hauptsächlich** *abends einkaufen.*   She goes shopping mainly in the evening.

German adverbs have no endings. Almost any German adjective can, without change, be used as an adverb. There are also many words that are adverbs only.

9.1 ADVERBS OF PLACE

Adverbs of place indicate location or direction. They determine the place of the action.

> *draußen* / outside
> *drinnen* / inside
> *droben* / up there
> *drüben* / over there
> *nirgends* / nowhere
> *überall* / everywhere
> *unterwegs* / on the way

EXAMPLES:

Draußen wartet jemand. / Someone is waiting outside.
Droben ist es zu warm. / It is too warm up there.
Ich habe drüben Verwandte. / I have relatives over there.
Das habe ich nirgends gesehen. / I have not seen that anywhere.

9.2 ADVERBS OF TIME

> *bald* / soon
> *dann* / then
> *endlich* / finally
> *gestern* / yesterday
> *heute* / today
> *inzwischen* / meanwhile
> *schließlich* / eventually
> *sofort* / right away

EXAMPLES:

Ich komme bald. / I am coming (will come) soon.
Dann ging ich nach Hause. / Then I went home.
Inzwischen rief ich ihn an. / Meanwhile, I called him.
Er kam sofort. / He came right away.

§9.3 ADVERBS OF MANNER AND DEGREE

Adverbs of manner and degree describe the way in which situation comes about or an activity occurs.

beinahe / almost
bereits / already
besonders / especially
etwa / maybe, about
ganz / quite
genug / enough
kaum / hardly
überdies / moreover
ziemlich / pretty, rather

EXAMPLES:
Er ist beinahe gestorben. / He almost died.
Sie ist etwa vierzig Jahre alt. / She is about forty years old.
Er ist ganz zufrieden damit. / He is quite satisfied with it.
Überdies raucht er zu viel. / Moreover, he smokes too much.
Der Film war ziemlich schlecht. / The film was pretty bad.

§9.4 ADVERBS INDICATING CAUTION

angeblich / allegedly
anscheinend / apparently
offenbar / obviously
scheinbar / on the face of it
vermutlich / presumably
wahrscheinlich / probably

EXAMPLES:
Angeblich war er Spion. / Allegedly he was a spy.
Offenbar tut er das gern. / Obviously he likes to do that.
Er hat vermutlich viel Geld. / Presumably he has a lot of mone

§9.5 ADVERBS WITH SUFFIXES

Adverbs with the Suffix *-weise*
begreiflicherweise / understandably
beispielsweise / for example
beziehungsweise / respectively
möglicherweise / possibly
schrittweise / step by step
versuchsweise / tentatively

EXAMPLES:
Begreiflicherweise kann ich das nicht erlauben. / Understand-
ably, I cannot permit that.
Dieser Film, beispielsweise, ist sehr gut. / This film, for exam
ple, is very good.

Wir werden das schrittweise durchgehen. / We will go through
  this step by step.

Adverbs with the Suffix *-maßen*
einigermaßen / to some extent *folgendermaßen* / as follows *gewissermaßen* / so to speak

EXAMPLES:
Ich stimme mit ihm einigermaßen überein. / I agree with him to
  some extent.
Er schreibt das folgendermaßen. / He writes as follows.
Wir sind gewissermaßen dafür verantwortlich. / We are respon-
  sible for it, so to speak.

§9.6 COMPARISON OF ADVERBS

Adjectives used as adverbs add *-er* in the comparative. In
the superlative they take *am,* and add *-en* to the stem of
the superlative.

Karl arbeitet schwer. / Karl works hard.
Kurt arbeitet schwerer. / Kurt works harder.
Otto arbeitet am schwersten. / Otto works hardest.

The same pattern: *am* + superlative + *-en* can also be used
for predicate adjectives:

Im Herbst ist das Wetter hier am schlechtesten. / In the fall,
  the weather here is the worst.

• The adverb *gern(e)* / gladly, willingly, is frequently used with
  a verb to denote *to like to:*
  EXAMPLES:
  Ich habe ihn gern. / I like him.
  Ich schwimme gern. / I like to swim.
  Er trinkt Wein gern. / He likes to drink wine.
  Er macht es gern. / He likes to do it.
  Ich helfe dir gern. / I like to help you.
  Er ist dort gern gesehen. / He is welcome there.
  Gern geschehen! / Don't mention it.

• The comparative form of *gern* is *lieber,* and the superlative
  is *am liebsten. Lieber* is translated as "(I'd) rather" or "(I)
  prefer"; *am liebsten* can be translated as *"like best."*
  EXAMPLES:
  Ich bleibe lieber zu Hause. / I prefer staying home.
  Ich ginge lieber ins Kino. I would rather go to the movies.
  Er bleibt am liebsten zu Hause. / He likes best to stay at home.

§9.7
MODAL
ADVERBS

Modal adverbs (also called intensifying or "flavoring" particles) are little words that lend color and emphasis to our speech. It is difficult in most instances to find the exact English equivalent for them.

German Word	Regular Meaning	Modal Usage
also	thus, therefore	*Also bis nächste Woche!* / Till next week then. *Also fangen wir an!* / Well, let's start.
denn	for, because	*Was ist denn los?* / Well, what's the matter? *Wieso denn?* / But why?
doch	however, yet	*Sie wird doch kommen?* / She will come, won't she?
ja	yes	*Komm ja nicht zu spät!* / Be sure not to be late.
noch	still, yet	*Ich habe ihn noch gestern gesehen.* / I saw him only yesterday.
nur	only	*Was können wir nur tun?* / What on earth can we do? *Sei nur vorsichtig!* / Do be careful.
schon	already	*Er kam schon am folgenden Tag.* / He came the very next day. *Das ist schon richtig, aber . . . /* That is correct, no doubt, but . . .
wohl	well	*Ob er das wohl weiß?* / I wonder if he knows that. *Er ist wohl krank.* / He probably is ill.

§10.

Prepositions

Prepositions are words that relate with other parts of speech to form phrases.

EXAMPLES:
*Brot ist **auf** dem Tisch.* / Bread is on the table.
*Er tut es **für** mich.* / He does it for me.

§10.1 PREPOSITIONAL CONTRACTIONS

Sometimes, prepositions and the definite article are combined in a single word. Here are some of the more common forms of these contractions:

> *an dem = am* / at the
> *an das = ans* / to the
> *auf das = aufs* / on the
> *bei dem = beim* / at the, by the
> *für das = fürs* / for the
> *in das = ins* / into the
> *in dem = im* / in the
> *um das = ums* / around the
> *von dem = vom* / from, of the
> *zu dem = zum* / to the
> *zu der = zur* / to the

EXAMPLES:
Am Abend gehen wir aus. / In the evening we go out.
*Er steht **beim** Fenster.* / He stands by the window.
*Sie geht **ins** Haus.* / She goes into the house.
*Ich erhielt das **vom** Lehrer.* / I received that from the teacher.
*Wir gingen **zur** Schule.* / We went to school.

§10.2 USAGE

In English, the noun in a prepositional phrase remains the same regardless of the preposition it follows. In German, the noun following a preposition is always in the accusative, the dative, or the genitive case.

§10.2–1 Prepositions Taking the Accusative

Preposition	Meaning	Example
bis	until, as far as	*Er wartete bis zwei Uhr.* / He waited until 2 o'clock. *Sie fährt bis München.* / She drives as far as Munich.

121

Preposition	Meaning	Example
durch	through, by	*Er ging durch den Park.* / He walked through the park. *Das Haus wurde durch Feuer zerstört.* / The house was destroyed by fire.
für	for	*Dieses Buch ist für ihn.* / This book is for him.
gegen	against, into, around, about	*Ich bin gegen den Krieg.* / I am against war. *Sie ist gegen den Zaun gefahren.* / She drove into the fence. *Wir hatten gegen hundert Besucher.* / We had around (about) one hundred visitors.
ohne	without	*Ich trinke Kaffee ohne Zucker.* / I drink coffee without sugar.
um	around, at	*Wir bauten eine Mauer um das Haus.* / We built a wall around the house. *Er kommt um zehn Uhr.* / He comes at ten o'clock.

§10.2–2 Prepositions Taking the Dative

Preposition	Meaning	Example
aus	out of, from, (made) of	*Er kommt gerade aus der Kirche.* / He is just coming out of church. *Herr Huber kommt aus Wien.* / Mr. Huber comes from Vienna. *Der Schmuck ist aus Silber.* / The jewelry is (made) of silver.
außer	except for, out of	*Außer meiner Schwester kenne ich niemand.* / Except for my sister, I don't know anybody. *Jetzt ist er außer Gefahr.* / Now he is out of danger.
bei	at, near, with	*Sie wohnt bei ihrer Mutter.* / She is living at her mother's. *Das Haus steht bei der Schule.* / The house is near the school. *Ich habe kein Kleingeld bei mir.* / I have no change with me.
gegenüber	across from	*Uns gegenüber ist ein Park.* / There is a park across from us.

Preposition	Meaning	Example
mit	with, by	*Ich arbeite mit ihm.* / I work with him. *Er kam mit dem Schiff an.* / He arrived by boat.
nach	after, to, according to	*Nach der Schule geht er schwimmen.* / After school he goes swimming. *Morgen fliegt er nach New York.* / He flies to New York tomorrow. *Dem Wörterbuch nach ist das richtig.* / According to the dictionary this is correct.
seit	since, for	*Seit vorigem Jahr wohnt er in Köln.* / He has been living in Cologne since last year. *Er arbeitet hier seit zwei Jahren.* / He has been working here for two years.
von	from, by, of	*Sie reist von Wien nach Salzburg.* / She travels from Vienna to Salzburg. *Das ist ein Roman von Hemingway.* / That is a novel by Hemingway. *Er ist ein Bekannter von mir.* / He is an acquaintance of mine.
zu (zum, zur)	to, at, for	*Er fährt zum Flughafen.* / He drives to the airport. *Er fuhr zur Kirche.* / He drove to church. *Wir sind zu Hause.* / We are at home. *Sie bekam das zu ihrem Geburtstag.* / She received this for her birthday.

Note: The adverbs *gegenüber* (across from) and *nach* (used in the sense of "according to") frequently follow the noun.

- *aus* and *von*

When indicating origin, *aus* means that one is either a native of a particular place or has been living there for some time; *von* means one has been in transit from a particular place.

EXAMPLES:

*Herr Müller kommt **aus** Bonn.* / Herr Müller comes from Bonn
*Herr Müller fuhr **von** Bonn nach Hamburg.* / Herr Müller drove
from Bonn to Hamburg.

> When getting something from a person, *von* is used;
> when getting something from a place, *aus* is used.

EXAMPLES:

*Er bekam ein Paket **von** seinem Sohn.* / He received a package
from his son.
*Dieses Paket kam **aus** Bonn.* / This package came *from* Bonn.

§10.2–3 Prepositions Taking the Dative or the Accusative

The dative is used to indicate a stable position or situation
It answers the question *wo* / where?

EXAMPLE:

*Die Katze sitzt **auf dem** Tisch.* / The cat sits *on* the table.
*(Wo sitzt die Katze? **Auf dem** Tisch.)*

The accusative is used to indicate a direction, a destination
or a motion toward a specific goal. It answers the question
wohin / whereto?

EXAMPLE:

*Die Katze springt **auf den** Tisch.* / The cat jumps *on*(to) the table
*(Wohin springt die Katze? **Auf den** Tisch.)*

Here we have movement toward a specific goal: the table

- The accusative is also used if the question is:

Über was / *worüber* / what about?

*Sie sprachen **über das** Buch.* / They talked about the book.

- Sometimes the dative is used if we can discern *no particular goal or destination:*

Er ist die ganze Zeit in der Stadt herumgelaufen. / He ran around town all day.

Preposition	Meaning	Preposition Taking the Dative	Preposition Taking the Accusative
an	at, by, on	*Der Student steht an der Tafel.* / The student stands at the blackboard.	*Er schreibt es an die Tafel.* / He writes it on the blackboard.
auf	on, onto	*Sie sitzt auf dem Sofa.* / She is sitting on the sofa.	*Er legt das Buch auf den Tisch.* / He is putting the book on the table.
hinter	behind	*Er steht hinter dem Haus.* / He is standing behind the house.	*Die Katze läuft hinter die Tür.* / The cat runs behind the door.
in	in, into, to	*Sie ist im (=in dem) Zimmer.* / She is in the room. *Hans ist in der Schule.* / Hans is in school.	*Sie geht ins (=in das) Zimmer.* / She walks into the room. *Hans geht in die Schule.* / Hans goes to school.
neben	beside	*Das Kind sitzt neben der Mutter.* / The child is sitting beside the mother.	*Setz dich neben den Vater!* / Sit down beside the father.
über	over (above), about	*Die Uhr hängt über dem Schreibtisch.* / The clock is hanging over (above) the desk.	*Hängen Sie die Uhr über den Schreibtisch!* / Hang the clock over the desk. *Wir sprachen über die Frau.* / We talked about the woman.
unter	under, below	*Sie liegt unter den Bäumen.* / She is lying under the trees.	*Das Kind lief unter den Baum.* / The child ran under the tree.
vor	in front of, before, ago	*Der Wagen steht vor der Tür.* / The car is standing in front of the door. *Das geschah vor dem Jahr 1941.* / That happened before 1941. *Das geschah vor vielen Jahren.* / That happened many years ago.	*Fahr den Wagen vor die Tür!* / Drive the car in front of the door.
zwischen	between	*Das Kind sitzt zwischen dem Herrn und der Dame.* / The child sits between the gentleman and the lady.	*Setz dich zwischen den Herrn und die Dame!* / Sit down between the gentleman and the lady.

§10.2–4 Prepositions Taking the Genitive

Preposition	Meaning	Example
(an)statt	instead of	*(An)statt eines Anzugs kaufte ich einen Mantel.* / I bought an overcoat instead of a suit.
innerhalb	within	*Er kommt innerhalb einer Stunde.* / He is coming within an hour.
jenseits	on the other side of	*Die Schule ist jenseits des Flusses.* / The school is on the other side of the river.
trotz	in spite of	*Trotz des Wetters ist mir nicht kalt.* / In spite of the weather I am not cold.
um . . . willen	for . . . sake	*Um Gottes willen!* / For God's sake!
während	during	*Er schläft während des Tages.* / He sleeps during the day.
wegen	because of	*Wegen seiner Verletzung kann er nicht Tennis spielen.* / Because of his injury he cannot play tennis. *Seiner Verletzung wegen kann er nicht Tennis spielen.*

Note: *wegen* can also follow the noun.

§11.

Conjunctions

Conjunctions are words that connect other words, phrases, or clauses.

An independent (or main) clause has at least one subject and one predicate and can stand by itself.

EXAMPLES:

Die Frau ist nett. / The woman is nice.
Sie ist hübsch. / She is pretty.

Die Frau ist nett,	*und*	*sie ist hübsch.* /
The woman is nice,	and	she is pretty.
↑	↑	↑

independent clause	conjunction	independent clause

11.1 COORDINATING CONJUNCTIONS

Conjunctions that join words, phrases, or independent clauses of equal standing are called *coordinating conjunctions.*

The principal coordinating conjunctions are:

> *aber* / but
> *oder* / or
> *sondern* / but, rather, on the contrary
> *und* / and

> Coordinating Conjunctions Joining Words

EXAMPLES:

Hans und Marie gingen ins Theater. / Hans and Marie went to the theater.
Du kannst Fleisch oder Fisch haben. / You may have meat or fish.
Sie ist dumm, aber schön. / She is stupid but beautiful.

> Coordinating Conjunctions Joining Phrases

EXAMPLES:

Er geht ins Kino, aber ich nicht. / He goes to the movies, but I don't.
Sie kommt oder vielleicht ihre Schwester. / She, or maybe her sister, is coming.

> Coordinating Conjunctions Joining Independent Clauses

EXAMPLES:

Alfred geht aus, und Otto bleibt zu Hause. / Alfred goes out, and Otto stays at home.

Der Vogel singt, und der Hund bellt. / The bird is singing, and the dog is barking.

Ich hörte ihn, aber er hörte mich nicht. / I heard him, but he did not hear me.

Sie ging nicht ins Kino, sondern (sie) blieb zu Hause. / She did not go to the movies but stayed at home.

Note: The coordinating conjunction *sondern* is used instead of *aber* when the preceding clause has a negative connotation, and then only when a wrong idea is replaced by a correct one.

• Some conjunctions come in pairs, such as "either—or," "neither—nor." Here are some examples.

EXAMPLES:

nicht nur — sondern auch / not only—but also
Nicht nur er, sondern auch seine Frau möchte kommen. / Not only he but also his wife wants to come.
sowohl — als auch / as well as
Sowohl er als auch sie waren hier. / He as well as she was here.
weder — noch / neither—nor
Weder Karl noch Otto ist dafür. / Neither Karl nor Otto is for it.
entweder — oder / either—or
Entweder zahlen Sie mir, oder ich verklage Sie. / Either you pay me, or I will sue you.

Note the inversion in the first clause (verb precedes subject) and normal word order in the second clause.

§11.2 SUBORDINATING CONJUNCTIONS

Conjunctions that make one clause dependent upon another clause are called *subordinating conjunctions.* They join dependent clauses to independent clauses or to other dependent clauses. A dependent clause cannot stand by itself.

• In English most subordinate clauses can be inverted without changing word order:
When I lived in Vienna, I often went to the theater.
I often went to the theater when I lived in Vienna.
• In German, too, the clauses can usually be inverted, but the word order often *does* change:
Als ich in Wien wohnte, ging ich oft ins Theater.
Ich ging oft ins Theater, als ich in Wien wohnte.

- Note that when the dependent clause *Als ich in Wien wohnte* precedes the main clause *ging ich oft ins Theater,* the word order changes from *ich ging* to *ging ich.*
- In dependent clauses introduced by a subordinating conjunction, the verb is at the end of the clause.

  EXAMPLE:
  Als er eintrat, stand jeder auf. / When he entered, everybody got up.

- For a more extensive discussion of word order, see Chapter 3.

11.2 – 1
he
onjunctions
enn, wann,
nd *indem* (or
adurch daß)

- The subordinating conjunction *wenn* is used to introduce a conditional clause.

  EXAMPLE:
  Wenn ich mehr Geld hätte, könnte ich mir ein Auto kaufen. / If I had more money, I could buy myself a car.

- It can also imply the future.

  EXAMPLE:
  Wenn er zurückkommt, wird er bei uns übernachten. / When he returns, he will stay with us overnight.

- Or it can express a repeated event.

  EXAMPLE:
  Wenn er kommt, besucht er uns immer. / Whenever he comes, he always visits us.

- *Wann* can be a subordinating conjunction.

  EXAMPLE:
  Ich weiß nicht, wann er kommt. / I don't know when he will come.

- Or it can be an interrogative pronoun.

  EXAMPLE:
  Wann geht er ins Büro? / When does he go to the office?

- The subordinate clause introduced by *indem* or *dadurch daß* explains the way something has been accomplished.

  EXAMPLES:
  Er bewies seine Freundschaft, indem er mir half.
  OR
  Er bewies seine Freundschaft, dadurch daß er mir half. / He proved his friendship by helping me.

- *Indem* (or *dadurch daß*) is usually expressed in English by a clause starting with "by" and using the gerund (the *-ing* ending of the verb).

§11.2-2
Other
Subordinating
Conjunctions

Here are some other subordinating conjunctions.

als ob / as though
bevor / before
da / since
daß / that
ob / whether, if
sobald / as soon as
soweit / as far as
weil / because

EXAMPLES:

Es sah aus, als ob es regnen würde. / It looked as though it would rain.

Bevor du ausgehst, mußt du das Geschirr waschen. / Before you go out, you have to wash the dishes.

Da ich noch Zeit hatte, rief ich ihn an. / Since I still had time, I called him.

Ich weiß, daß sie klug ist. / I know that she is clever.

Weißt du, ob er da ist? / Do you know whether he is here?

Sobald ich ihn sehe, rufe ich Sie an. / As soon as I see him, I'll call you.

Soweit ich informiert bin, geht es ihm gut. / As far as I know, is all right.

Ich bin in die Berge gefahren, weil das Wetter schön war. / I drove to the mountains because the weather was nice.

§12.

Word Formation

A most productive feature of the German language is its capacity to form new words from two or more independent words or to add prefixes and suffixes. The new word that then emerges often represents an independent unit with a meaning all its own. *Baumschule* (nursery) is not the place where trees go to school, *Handtücher* (towels) are not specifically reserved for your hands; and *Junggesellen* (bachelors) need not necessarily be young.

§12.1 COMPOUND-ING INDEPEN-DENT WORDS

Compound nouns are produced by putting together two or more words; the last noun determines the gender and the number of the new word. The words preceding the last noun modify it. Modifying elements can be nouns, adjectives, verbs, adverbs, prepositions, and numerals. For more on compound nouns, see §4.2–3.

Nouns
der Birnbaum / the pear tree *die Landwirtschaftslehre* / the agricultural science
Adjectives
der Rotfink / the bullfinch *das Gelbfieber* / the yellow fever
Verbs
das Sehrohr / the telescope *die Sehnsucht* / the nostalgia
Adverbs
die Jetztzeit / the present *die Wiederbelebung* / the revival
Prepositions
der Absatz / the paragraph *die Zulage* / the extra pay
Numerals
die Hundertjahrfeier / the centennial *der Dreifuß* / the tripod

- In linking compound nouns, the connecting letter -s- is inserted after the noun suffixes -heit, -ing, -ion, -keit, -schaft, -tät, -tum, and -ung.

  EXAMPLES:
  die Freiheitsliebe / the love of freedom
  das Lieblingsbuch / the favorite book
  die Präzisionswaage / the precision balance
  die Gesellschaftsfahrt / the conducted tour
  die Relativitätstheorie / the theory of relativity

- The connecting letters -s- or -es- follow a masculine or neuter modifying noun.

  EXAMPLES:
  der Landsmann / the compatriot
  die Tagesordnung / the agenda
  die Schiffsküche / the galley
  das Schweinsleder / the pigskin

- The connecting letter -s- follows a feminine modifying noun.

  EXAMPLES:
  der Geburtstag / the birthday
  der Geschichtsprofessor / the history professor
  das Hilfsmittel / the remedy
  das Hochzeitsgeschenk / the wedding present

- In some compounds the connecting letter -n- is used following a feminine noun.

  EXAMPLES:
  das Eichenlaub / the oak leaves
  der Scheibenwischer / the window wiper
  die Sonnenfinsternis / the eclipse of the sun
  der Wochentag / the weekday

§12.2 COMPOUND-ING WITH PREFIXES

§12.2–1 Nouns and Adjectives

Prefix	Meaning	Examples
Ge-	Denotes a concept of collectivity.	das Gebäck / pastry das Gebirge / mountains das Gemüse / vegetables
Miß-	Changes the meaning of a word into its opposite. Accent is on the first syllable.	die Mißhandlung / maltreatment der Mißmut / discontent das Mißtrauen / mistrust

Prefix	Meaning	Examples
Rück-	Means going back.	*die Rückäußerung* / reply *der Rückfall* / relapse *die Rückkehr* / return *der Rückschluß* / conclusion
Un-	Indicates negation or the opposite. Sometimes also intensifies the meaning of the word.	*der Undank* / ingratitude *undankbar* / ungrateful *der Ungehorsam* / disobedience *ungehorsam* / disobedient *das Unglück* / misfortune *unglücklich* / unhappy
Ur-	Denotes origin, originality, or a primitive state.	*der Urbewohner* / native *das Urbild* / prototype *der Urzustand* / primitive state
Wohl-	Denotes the good, the healthy, the happy.	*das Wohlbefinden* / good health *das Wohlbehagen* / comfort *die Wohlfahrt* / welfare *das Wohlwollen* / goodwill *die Wohlstandsgesellschaft* / affluent society *wohlbekannt* / well-known *wohlerzogen* / well-bred

12.2–2
Verb Prefixes

See §8.6–4 and §8.6–5 on the more common verbs with separable and inseparable prefixes. In this section some of the inseparable verb prefixes are discussed.

- The verb prefix *be-* turns an intransitive verb into a transitive verb.

   EXAMPLES:

wohnen / to live (intransitive)   *bewohnen* / to inhabit (transitive)   *Ich wohne in einem Haus.* / I live in a house.   *Ich bewohne ein Haus.* / I inhabit a house.
weinen / to weep (intransitive)   *beweinen* / to mourn (transitive)   *Ich weine über etwas.* / I weep about something.   *Ich beweine meinen Vater.* / I weep for my father.

Here are some other verb prefixes:

Prefix	Meaning	Examples
ent-	Denotes either separation or the start of something	*entarten* / to degenerate *entblößen* / to uncover *entdecken* / to discover *enteignen* / to expropriate *entfernen* / to remove
er-	Can denote the start of something new or the result of an action.	*erfinden* / to invent *erforschen* / to investigate *erkennen* / to recognize *ermöglichen* / to make possible *erschließen* / to make accessible
ver-	Indicates either action in a negative sense, identification of an action, or a shift into a different state.	*verarbeiten* / to process *verarmen* / to become poor *verbergen* / to conceal *verbrauchen* / to use up *verhungern* / to starve
zer-	Indicates crushing, tearing, or breaking apart of something.	*zerbrechen* / to break to pieces *zerdrücken* / to crush *zerfallen* / to fall apart *zermahlen* / to grind down *zerreißen* / to tear up

§12.3 COMPOUNDING WITH SUFFIXES
§12.3 – 1 Masculine Nouns

Suffix	Meaning	Examples
el-	Often denotes tools or instruments.	*der Flügel* / wing *der Hebel* / lever *der Säbel* / sword *der Stachel* / thorn *der Schlüssel* / key
-er	Characterizes a person, or indicates place of origin.	*der Amerikaner* / American *der Ansager* / announcer *der Bäcker* / baker *der Lehrer* / teacher *der Witwer* / widower
-ling	Denotes a person's condition. Some of the words have a pejorative meaning; a few take the umlaut.	*der Emporkömmling* / upstart *der Feigling* / coward *der Flüchtling* / refugee *der Liebling* / darling *der Säugling* / infant

EXCEPTIONS:

die Schaufel / shovel
die Windel / diaper
die Schaukel / swing

Suffix	Meaning	Examples
-e	Forms mostly abstract nouns from verbs and adjectives, often with an umlaut.	die Flechte / braid, twist die Gabe / gift die Güte / goodness die Hilfe / help die Höhe / height
-ei	Indicates places of business and occupation. Some of the words have a derogatory connotation. The accent is always on the -ei.	die Brauerei / brewery die Bücherei / library die Druckerei / print shop die Schmeichelei / flattery die Schreiberei / scribbling
-heit	Designates a condition.	die Freiheit / freedom die Kindheit / childhood die Menschheit / mankind die Schönheit / beauty die Wahrheit / truth
-keit	Used following the suffixes -bar, -ig, -lich, -sam, and sometimes also after -el and -er. It often denotes a character trait.	die Dankbarkeit / gratitude die Großzügigkeit / generosity die Heiterkeit / cheerfulness die Sauberkeit / cleanliness die Traurigkeit / sadness
-schaft	Indicates a condition, territory, or a collective group	die Arbeiterschaft / working class die Freundschaft / friendship die Landschaft / landscape die Ortschaft / locality, village
-ung	Denotes the consequences of an action.	die Beerdigung / burial die Erziehung / education die Genugtuung / satisfaction die Hoffnung / hope die Versicherung / insurance
-ion	Formed with nouns of foreign origin. The accent is on the last syllable.	die Lektion / lesson die Nation / nation die Revolution / revolution die Situation / situation die Station / station
-tät	Also formed with nouns of foreign origin. The accent is on the last syllable.	die Aktivität / activity die Elektrizität / electricity die Humanität / humanity die Qualität / quality die Universität / university

EXCEPTIONS:
der Glaube / belief
der Wille / will

§12.3–3
Neuter Nouns

Suffix	Meaning	Examples
-chen	This is a diminutive denoting littleness or endearment. The umlaut occurs frequently.	*das Häuschen* / little house *das Hündchen* / little dog *das Kindchen* / little child
-lein	Same as above. This suffix is less common today.	*das Brüderlein* / little brother *das Tischlein* / little table
-nis	Denotes the result of something.	*das Ergebnis* / result *das Erzeugnis* / product *das Gefängnis* / prison *das Gelöbnis* / pledge
-sal	Results in abstract nouns.	*das Labsal* / comfort *das Schicksal* / fate *das Wirrsal* / confusion
-sel	Has a diminutive effect.	*das Anhängsel* / pendant *das Rätsel* / riddle *das Überbleibsel* / re-mainder
-tum	Denotes historical entities, collective units, or abstract ideas.	*das Altertum* / antiquity *das Brauchtum* / folklore *das Christentum* / Christen-dom *das Eigentum* / property *das Priestertum* / priesthood

> EXCEPTIONS:
> *die Kenntnis* / knowledge
> *der Irrtum* / error
> *der Reichtum* / wealth

§12.3–4
Adjectives

Suffix	Meaning	Examples
-bar	Denotes something that can be done or is obvious.	*fruchtbar* / fertile *sichtbar* / visible *sonderbar* / strange *unverkennbar* / unmistakable
-er	Denotes origin from a city.	*Wiener* / Viennese *Münchner* / from Munich *New Yorker* / from New York
-(e)n, -ern	These suffixes are used with materials.	*golden* / gold(en) *kupfern* / copper *papieren* / paper *seiden* / silk(en) *wollen* / wool(len)

Suffix	Meaning	Examples
-haft	Denotes the manner in which a person acts or appears to be.	*fabelhaft* / fabulous *krankhaft* / morbid *laienhaft* / amateurish *mädchenhaft* / girlish *schwatzhaft* / talkative
-ig	Denoting characterization or condition.	*findig* / resourceful *freudig* / joyful *günstig* / favorable *schmutzig* / dirty
-isch	Comparable to the English -ish or -ic, it indicates attributes, characteristics, or the place of origin.	*amerikanisch* / American *englisch* / English *musikalisch* / musical *närrisch* / foolish *tragisch* / tragic
-lich	Denotes certain qualities or characteristics.	*freundlich* / friendly *gefährlich* / dangerous *herzlich* / cordial *jugendlich* / youthful *kleinlich* / petty
-sam	Denotes attributes of living beings.	*arbeitsam* / industrious *fügsam* / docile *furchtsam* / timid *gemeinsam* / common *strebsam* / ambitious

Differences in meaning between adjectives ending in -*lich* and those ending in -*ig*:

geistlich / sacred
geistig / intellectual
geschäftlich /commercial
geschäftig / busy
mündlich / oral
mündig / of age
verständlich / comprehensible
verständig / reasonable

Differences in meaning between adjectives ending in -*lich* and those ending in -*isch:*

heimlich / secret
heimisch / domestic
kindlich / childlike
kindisch / childish
weiblich / feminine
weibisch / effeminate

§12.3–5 Adjectives as Suffixes

Suffix	Meaning	Examples
-arm	Lacking in something.	*blútarm* / anemic *blutárm* / very poor *wasserarm* / lacking in water
-fähig	Able to do something.	*arbeitsfähig* / able-bodied *konkurrenzfähig* / competitive *lebensfähig* / viable
-los	Free of something (comparable to the English -less).	*arbeitslos* / unemployed *hilflos* / helpless *sprachlos* / speechless
-mäßig	In accordance with something.	*ebenmäßig* / well proportioned *gleichmäßig* / constant *ordnungsmäßig* / orderly
-reich	Rich in something.	*arbeitsreich* / busy *einflußreich* / influential *ereignisreich* / eventful
-voll	Full of something (comparable to the English -ful).	*geheimnisvoll* / mysterious *liebevoll* / affectionate *grauenvoll* / dreadful
-wert	Worth something.	*hörenswert* / worth listening to *lesenswert* / worth reading *sehenswert* / worth seeing
-würdig	Worthy of something.	*denkwürdig* / memorable *glaubwürdig* / credible *merkwürdig* / noteworthy

Special Topics

§13.

Common Phrases and Idiomatic Expressions

The following turns of expression are helpful.

alles und nichts / all and nothing
alle zwei Tage / every other day *alles in allem* / on the whole, all told *nichts dergleichen* / nothing of the kind *für nichts und wieder nichts* / for no reason at all *Nichts zu machen!* / Nothing doing!

EXAMPLES:

Ich habe nichts dergleichen gehört. / I have heard nothing of the kind.

Alles in allem bin ich damit zufrieden. / All told, I am satisfied with it.

Er trifft ihn alle zwei Tage. / He meets him every other day.

gestern, heute und morgen / yesterday, today, and tomorrow
gestern abend / last night *heute abend* / tonight *heute morgen* / this morning *heute über eine Woche* / a week from today *morgen früh* / tomorrow morning

EXAMPLES:

Gestern abend ging ich ins Konzert. / Last night I went to the concert.

Heute morgen fahre ich nach Frankfurt. / This morning I'll drive to Frankfurt.

Morgen früh rufe ich dich an. / I'll call you tomorrow morning.

immer und nie / always and never
immer mehr / more and more *immer weniger* / less and less *immer wieder* / again and again *fast nie* / hardly ever *nie wieder* / no more, never again

139

EXAMPLES:

Er erzählt mir immer wieder den gleichen Witz. / He tells me the same joke again and again.

Ich habe immer weniger Lust darauf. / I feel like it less and less.

Er besucht ihn fast nie. / He hardly ever visits him.

noch / still, yet
noch immer / still *noch nicht* / not yet *noch jetzt* / even now *noch dazu* / what's more *noch einmal* / once more

EXAMPLES:

Wir sind noch immer hier. / We are still here.

Sie ist noch nicht gekommen. / She has not come yet.

Er versucht es noch einmal. / He is trying it once more.

Tag und Nacht / day and night
dieser Tage / the other day *den ganzen Tag* / all day long *Tags darauf* / the day after, the next day *vergangene Nacht* / last night *die ganze Nacht hindurch* / all night long

EXAMPLES:

Dieser Tage habe ich sie besucht. / I visited her the other day.

Tags darauf kam er zu mir. / He came to me the next day.

Er arbeitete die ganze Nacht hindurch. / He worked all night long

Zeit / time
auf Zeit / on credit *die ganze Zeit* / all the time *Es ist höchste Zeit.* / It is high time. *in kürzester Zeit* / in no time *in letzter Zeit* / lately

EXAMPLES:

Er kauft alles auf Zeit. / He buys everything on credit.

Es ist höchste Zeit, daß sie kommt. / It is high time that she came

In letzter Zeit fühle ich mich nicht wohl. / Lately I don't feel well

**13.2
IDIOMATIC
EXPRESSIONS**

Idioms are forms of expression in grammatical construction and phraseology that are peculiar to a people. Being unique in style and structure, they resist literal translation except in those rare instances when precisely the same idiom exists in two different languages. Idioms enrich the language and enhance its expressiveness by adding color and a distinct flavor.

Expressions with the verb *sein* (to be)

Er ist im sieb(en)ten Himmel. / He is walking on air. (He is in seventh heaven.)
Das ist mir zu hoch. / That is beyond me.
Er ist kerngesund. / He is as fit as a fiddle.

Expressions with the verb *haben* (to have)

Sie hat Grütze im Kopf. / She has brains.
Er hat die Nase voll davon. / He is fed up with it.
Er hat Geld wie Heu. / He is loaded (with money).

Expressions with the verb *gehen* (to go)

Es ging wie am Schnürchen. / It went like clockwork.
Das geht auf meine Rechnung. / This one is on me.
Er geht in die Luft. / He flies into a rage.

Expressions with the verb *kommen* (to come)

Der kommt auf keinen grünen Zweig. / He'll never make the grade.
Er kommt nicht vom Fleck. / He makes no headway.
Er kommt vom Hundertsten ins Tausendste. / He goes off on a tangent.

Expressions with the verb *liegen* (to lie)

An wem liegt es? / Whose fault is it?
Es liegt mir sehr viel daran. / It matters a great deal to me.
Das liegt mir nicht. / That's not in my line.

Expressions with the verb *machen* (to make)

Er macht gute Miene zum bösen Spiel. / He makes the best ❪
a bad situation.
Mach dir nichts draus! / Don't lose any sleep over it.
Sie macht sich Luft. / She lets off steam.

Expressions with the verb *nehmen* (to take)

Er nimmt die Folgen auf sich. / He is facing the music.
Sie läßt es sich nicht nehmen. / She won't be talked out of it
Wie man's nimmt. / That depends.

Expressions with the verb *reden* (to talk)

Er redet sich heiser. / He talks a mile a minute.
Du hast leicht reden. / It is easy for you to talk.
Darüber läßt sich reden. / That's a possibility.

Expressions with the verb *sagen* (to say)

Das hat nichts zu sagen. / That makes no difference.
Er hat ihm seine Meinung gesagt. / He gave him a piece of h❪
mind.
Die Generäle haben jetzt das Sagen. / The generals now sa❪
what goes.

Expressions with the verb *sitzen* (to sit)

Das sitzt ihm wie angegossen. / That fits him like a glove.
Jetzt sitzt er in der Tinte. / Now he is in the soup.
Das hat gesessen! / That hit home.

Expressions with the verb *stehen* (to stand)

Er steht in der Kreide. / He is in the red.
Es steht schlecht um ihn. / He is in a bad way.
Er steht seinen Mann. / He stands his ground.

Expressions with the verb *stellen* (to put, to place)

Wie stellen Sie sich dazu? / What do you say to this?
Er stellt sich dumm. / He plays the fool.
Er ist auf sich selbst gestellt. / He is on his own.

§13.3
MISCELLA-
NEOUS
EXPRESSIONS

The following is a short list of miscellaneous expressions that should prove useful.

> *abgesehen davon* / apart from that
> *Einen Augenblick, bitte.* / One moment, please.
> *Das ist ausgeschlossen.* / That is out of the question.
> *Das ist schade.* / That's a pity.
> *Er lernt es auswendig.* / He learns it by heart.
> *Es steht nicht dafür.* / It is not worth it.
> *ehrlich gesagt* / frankly speaking
> *Das geht mich nichts an.* / That's none of my business.
> *Gern geschehen!* / Don't mention it.
> *Die Reihe ist an mir.* / It is my turn.

EXAMPLES:

Abgesehen davon, bin ich daran nicht interessiert. / Apart from that, I am not interested in it.

Er muß das Gedicht auswendig lernen. / He has to learn the poem by heart.

Ehrlich gesagt, bin ich froh, daß er nicht kommt. / Frankly speaking, I am glad that he is not coming.

Vielen Dank für Ihre Hilfe. Gern geschehen! / Many thanks for your help. Don't mention it.

Wo spielen wir nächstens? Die Reihe ist an mir. / Where are we playing next time? It is my turn.

§14.

Numbers

Cardinal numbers indicate a precise quantity. They are used for counting. The numbers from zero to twenty are as follows:

Zero to Twenty			
0	*null*		
1	*eins*	11	*elf*
2	*zwei*	12	*zwölf*
3	*drei*	13	*dreizehn*
4	*vier*	14	*vierzehn*
5	*fünf*	15	*fünfzehn*
6	*sechs*	16	*sechzehn*
7	*sieben*	17	*siebzehn*
8	*acht*	18	*achtzehn*
9	*neun*	19	*neunzehn*
10	*zehn*	20	*zwanzig*

- Numbers from one to nine are called *Einer* (ones); ten, twenty, thirty, etc., are called *Zehner* (tens).
- Numbers from twenty-one on are formed by the *Einer,* followed by the word *und* (and), followed by the *Zehner:*

  einundzwanzig / twenty-one (literally, one and twenty)
  neunundneunzig / ninety-nine (literally, nine and ninety)

Twenty to One Hundred		
20 *zwanzig*	61	*einundsechzig*
21 *einundzwanzig*	62	*zweiundsechzig*
22 *zweiundzwanzig*		. . .
. . .	70	*siebzig*
30 *dreißig*	71	*einundsiebzig*
31 *einunddreißig*	72	*zweiundsiebzig*
32 *zweiunddreißig*		. . .
. . .	80	*achtzig*
40 *vierzig*	81	*einundachtzig*
41 *einundvierzig*	82	*zweiundachtzig*
42 *zweiundvierzig*		. . .
. . .	90	*neunzig*
50 *fünfzig*	91	*einundneunzig*
51 *einundfünfzig*	92	*zweiundneunzig*
52 *zweiundfünfzig*		. . .
. . .	100	*hundert (einhundert)*
60 *sechzig*		

- In numbers from 101 on, *und* is not used between hundreds (or thousands) and ones, or between hundreds (or thousands) and tens.

One Hundred to One Hundred Thousand	
100 *hundert*	1 000 *tausend (eintausend)*
101 *hunderteins*	1 001 *tausendeins*
102 *hundertzwei*	1 002 *tausendzwei*
. . .	. . .
200 *zweihundert*	1 200 *eintausendzweihun-*
. . .	*dert* OR *zwölfhundert*
210 *zweihundertzehn*	. . .
. . .	100 000 *hunderttausend*

- Groups of three digits are separated by a space. Numbers of less than one million are written as one word.

  EXAMPLES:
  dreiundsiebzigtausendvierhundertzweiundachtzig / 73 482
  achthundertfünfundsiebzigtausenddreihundertzweiundvierzig
  875 342

Million, Billion, Trillion	
1 000 000	*eine Million*
1 000 000 000	*eine Milliarde*
1 000 000 000 000	*eine Billion*

- The German *Milliarde* is the same as the American billion; the American trillion is equivalent to the German *Billion.*

- Numbers of a million or more are not written as one word:

  zwei Millionen siebenhunderttausend / 2 700 000

- Please note that *Million, Milliarde,* and *Billion* are feminine.

  EXAMPLES:
  London hat mehr als acht Millionen Einwohner. / London has more than eight million inhabitants.
  Das Außenhandelsdefizit der Vereinigten Staaten beträgt viele Milliarden / The foreign trade deficit of the United States amounts to many billions.

§14.1–1
The Number "One" (ein, eins, eine)

- The word *ein* (followed by *und*) is used to form the numerals 21, 31, etc.

  EXAMPLES:
  einundvierzig / 41
  einundachtzig / 81

- The word *eins* is used to form the numerals 101, 201, 1001, etc.; it is placed at the end of the compound number and is not preceded by *und*.

  EXAMPLES:
  dreihunderteins / 301
  zweitausendeins / 2 001

- When used as a numerical adjective or pronoun, the stem *ein-* takes the same endings as the demonstrative stem *dies-* (as in *diese;* see §5.4).

  EXAMPLES:
  Der **eine** *Mann, den ich kannte, war nicht hier.* / The one man whom I knew was not here.
  Einer *von ihnen kam mit.* / One of them came along.

- *Ein* does not take any endings when introducing a fraction; when preceding the noun *Uhr*, indicating time; or when followed by *oder, bis,* or *und (der-, die-) dasselbe.*

  EXAMPLES:
  Er multipliziert drei Fünftel mit **ein** *Sechstel.* / He multiplies three-fifths by one-sixth.
  Ich traf ihn nach **ein** *Uhr.* / I met him after one o'clock.
  Die Ware kommt in **ein** *oder zwei Tagen an.* / The merchandise will arrive in one or two days.
  Er muß **ein** *bis zwei Monate warten.* / He must wait one to two months.
  Das ist **ein** *und dasselbe.* / That is one and the same (thing).

§14.1–2
Repetitive and Duplicating Numbers

- *Repetitive numbers* indicate how many times something is repeated. They are formed by adding the suffix *-mal* to the cardinal number.

  EXAMPLES:
  Ich sah ihn zweimal. / I saw him twice.
  Er hat mir dreimal geschrieben. / He wrote to me three times.

- By adding the suffix *-malig* to the cardinal number, we can form adjectives: *ein-, einmalig.*

EXAMPLES:

Das ist eine einmalige Gelegenheit. / This is a unique opportunity.
Dieser Film ist etwas Einmaliges. / This film is something singular.

- *Duplicating numbers* are adjectives that can be formed from cardinal numbers by adding the suffix *-fach.*

  EXAMPLES:

  Schreiben Sie die Rechnung in dreifacher Ausfertigung. / Write the invoice in triplicate.
  Die Preise stiegen aufs Zehnfache. / The prices rose tenfold.

- *Zweifach* is often replaced by *doppelt* (double, twofold).

  EXAMPLE:

  Die Preise sind ums doppelte gestiegen. / The prices doubled.

14.2 ORDINAL NUMBERS

Ordinal numbers refer to positions in a sequence or series. They are, in most cases, declined the same way as other adjectives.

der, die, das		
1st *erste*	13th	*dreizehnte*
2nd *zweite*	14th	*vierzehnte*
3rd *dritte*	15th	*fünfzehnte*
4th *vierte*	16th	*sechzehnte*
5th *fünfte*	17th	*siebzehnte*
6th *sechste*	18th	*achtzehnte*
7th *siebente* (or *siebte*)	19th	*neunzehnte*
8th *achte*	20th	*zwanzigste*
9th *neunte*	. . .	
10th *zehnte*	100th	*hundertste*
11th *elfte*	. . .	
12th *zwölfte*	1 000th	*tausendste*

- Ordinal numbers written as numbers always have a period after them.

  EXAMPLES:

  der 1.; der erste / the first
  der 2.; der zweite / the second
  der 30.; der dreißigste / the thirtieth
  der 100.; der hundertste / the hundredth
  Heinrich VIII.; Heinrich der Achte / Henry VIII
  Elisabeth II.; Elisabeth die Zweite / Elizabeth II

- Ordinal numbers are used in classifying. They indicate a certain sequence:

  1. *erstens* / first(ly) (in the first place)
  2. *zweitens* / second(ly) (in the second place)
  3. *drittens* / third(ly) (in the third place)

Ich sehe mir einen Film lieber im Fernsehen als im Kino an,	I'd rather watch a film on TV than on the big screen
1. *(erstens) kostet das weniger,*	first, it costs less,
2. *(zweitens) muß ich nicht ausgehen und*	second, I don't have to go out, and
3. *(drittens) kann ich mich dabei mit meiner Frau unterhalten.*	third, I can talk with my wife while watching it.

- The denominators of fractions are formed from ordinal numbers by adding the ending -*el* to the stem of the ordin
  $\frac{1}{3}$ = *ein Drittel*　　　　$\frac{5}{100}$ = *fünf Hundertstel*
  $\frac{1}{4}$ = *ein Viertel*　　　　$\frac{7}{1000}$ = *sieben Tausendstel*
  $\frac{3}{17}$ = *drei Siebzehntel*

- *halb-* (half), *Hälfte* (half), *anderthalb* (one and a half), *zweieinhalb* (two and one-half).

  EXAMPLES:
  Sie hat den halben Kuchen gegessen. / She ate half the cake
  Die andere Hälfte gehört mir. / The other half is mine.
  Ich habe anderthalb Stunden auf dich gewartet. / I waited for you for one and a half hours.
  Er kommt in zweieinhalb Jahren zurück. / He will come back i two and a half years.

§14.3 MISCELLA-NEOUS TERMS

In German, decimal numbers are written with a comma, n a period.

> 5,6 *(fünf Komma sechs)* = 5.6
> 48,60 *(achtundvierzig Komma sechzig)* = 48.60
> 0,7 *(null Komma sieben)* = 0.7

EXAMPLES:
Das Zimmer ist 6,5 Meter (m) lang und 5,6 m breit. / The roo is 6.5 meters (m) long and 5.6 m wide.
Das kostet DM 18,50. / That costs DM 18.50.
Das kostet achtzehn Mark fünfzig. / That costs eighteen mar (and) fifty (pfennigs).

Some Mathematical Expressions

der Grad / degree	*addieren* / to add
der Kreis / circle	*subtrahieren* / to subtract
das Dreieck / triangle	*multiplizieren* / to multiply
das Viereck / rectangle	*dividieren* / to divide
das Quadrat / square	

EXAMPLES:

Das Thermometer steht auf null Grad. / The thermometer is at zero degrees.

mit fünf multiplizieren / to multiply by five

durch zwei dividieren / to divide by two

A Little Arithmetic·

Sechs plus acht gleich (ist) vierzehn.	$6 + 8 = 14$
Zwanzig minus (weniger) zwölf gleich acht.	$20 - 12 = 8$
Acht mal neun gleich (ist) zweiundsiebzig.	$8 \times 9 = 72$
Dreißig geteilt durch sechs gleich fünf.	$30 \div 6 = 5$
Fünf hoch zwei (fünf Quadrat) gleich fünfundzwanzig.	$5^2 = 25$

§15.

Telling Time

15.1
WHAT TIME IS IT?

In German you can ask this question in the following ways

> *Wie spät ist es?*
> *Wieviel Uhr ist es?*

- When designating time, the word *Uhr* (clock) is always in the singular:

    Es ist vier Uhr./ It is four o'clock.

- The word *Zeit* (time) is not used to ask the time; it expresses an abstract concept.

    Wie die Zeit vergeht!/ How time flies!
    Zeit ist Geld./ Time is money.

§15.2
THE HOURS

§15.2–1
The Twelve-Hour Clock

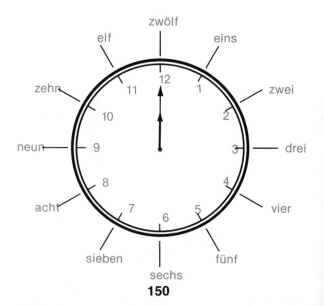

150

In ordinary conversation you can distinguish the different times of day by using the following expressions:

> *morgens (am Morgen)* / in the morning
> *mittags (zu Mittag)* / at noon
> *vormittags* / before noon
> *nachmittags (am Nachmittag)* / in the afternoon
> *abends (am Abend)* / in the evening
> *um Mitternacht* / at midnight
> *nachts* / at night

EXAMPLES:

Es ist sechs Uhr morgens./ It is 6 A.M.
Es ist zwölf Uhr mittags./ It is 12 P.M. (noon).
Es ist acht Uhr abends./ It is 8 P.M.

Here are some other useful phrases:

Es ist Punkt neun./ It is nine o'clock sharp.
Er trifft mich Schlag sieben Uhr./ He meets me on the stroke of seven.
Es ist ungefähr (zirka, gegen) neun Uhr./ It is about nine o'clock.

15.2–2
The Twenty-Four-Hour Clock

The twenty-four-hour clock, in German called *Bahnzeit* (railroad time), is the official time system in Germany. It is used for television and radio schedules, for all public events, for store and office hours, and for timetables (bus, air, rail). It is more practical than the twelve-hour system since it makes the German equivalents of A.M. and P.M. (*morgens, abends, vormittags, nachmittags,* etc.) unnecessary.

- According to German *Bahnzeit,* the hours after noon are as follows:

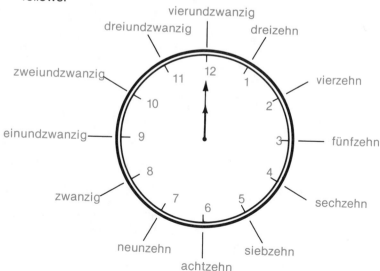

EXAMPLES:

Es ist dreizehn Uhr. / It is 1 P.M. (13:00).
Es ist sechzehn Uhr. / It is 4 P.M. (16:00).
Es ist einundzwanzig Uhr. / It is 9 P.M. (21:00).
Es ist vierundzwanzig Uhr. / It is 12 midnight (24:00 indicates the end of the day).
Es ist null Uhr. / It is 12 midnight (00.00 indicates the beginning of a day).

§15.3
THE MINUTES

- Minutes *(die Minuten)* may be added directly after the hour as in English.

  EXAMPLES:

  Es ist acht Uhr fünf. / It is eight-oh-five (8:05).
  Es ist dreizehn Uhr dreizehn. / It is thirteen-thirteen (1:13 P.M.)

- Or they may be used with the word *nach* (after, past).

  EXAMPLES:

  Es ist zehn (Minuten) nach acht. / It is ten (minutes) past eight.
  Es ist achtzehn nach sechs. / It is eighteen past six.

- As the next hour approaches, you may use *vor* or *in* (to, before) to express minutes.

  EXAMPLES:

  Es ist zwölf vor elf. / It is twelve to (of, before) eleven.
  Es ist fünf vor vierzehn. / It is five to (of, before) fourteen (2 P.M.)
  Es ist in drei Minuten sieben. / It is three minutes before seven.

- To express half and quarter hours, the words *halb* (half), *Viertel* (quarter), and *dreiviertel* (three-quarters) are used.

  Es ist halb neun. / It is half past eight (literally, half [toward] nine).
  Es ist halb eins. / It is half past twelve (literally, half [toward] one).
  Es ist (ein) Viertel vor neun. / It is a quarter to nine.

  Here *Viertel* is capitalized because it is a noun.

  Es ist dreiviertel fünf. / It is a quarter to five (literally, three-quarters [toward] five).

  Here *dreiviertel* is spelled with a small *d* because it is a fraction, used as an adjective.

- Be careful when using *Bahnzeit*. Use hours and minutes only. Do *not* use *halb, Viertel,* or *dreiviertel.*

  EXAMPLES:

  Das Kino fängt um achtzehn dreißig an. / The movie starts at 6:30 P.M. (18:30).

  Das Fußballspiel beginnt um fünfzehn fünfundvierzig. / The football game starts at 3:45 P.M. (15:45).

§16.

Days, Months, Seasons, Dates, and the Weather

16.1
THE DAYS
OF THE WEEK

Die Tage der Woche are:

> *der Sonntag* / Sunday
> *der Montag* / Monday
> *der Dienstag* / Tuesday
> *der Mittwoch* / Wednesday
> *der Donnerstag* / Thursday
> *der Freitag* / Friday
> *der Samstag*
>
> **OR**
>
> *der Sonnabend* / Saturday

Note: *Sonnabend* is sometimes used in Northern Germany.

EXAMPLES:

Am Sonntag spiele ich Fußball. / On Sunday I will play football
Holst du mich nächsten Dienstag ab? / Will you pick me up ne
Tuesday?
Ich besuche meine Schwester jeden Freitag. / I visit my sister
every Friday.

§16.2
THE MONTHS
OF THE YEAR

Die Monate des Jahres are:

der Januar / January	*der Juli* / July
der Februar / February	*der August* / August
der März / March	*der September* / September
der April / April	*der Oktober* / October
der Mai / May	*der November* / November
der Juni / June	*der Dezember* / December

Note: *Jänner,* instead of *Januar,* is often used in Southe
Germany, Austria, and Switzerland. *Feber,* instead of
Februar, is frequently used in Austria.

EXAMPLES:

Februar ist der kürzeste Monat des Jahres. / February is the
shortest month of the year.
Im Juli oder im August geht man gern auf Urlaub. / In July or i
August people like to take their vacation.

154

Im November ist es meistens kalt und regnerisch. / In November it is cold and rainy most of the time.

16.3
THE SEASONS

Die Jahreszeiten are:

> *der Frühling (das Frühjahr)* / spring
> *der Sommer* / summer
> *der Herbst* / autumn
> *der Winter* / winter

EXAMPLES:

Im Frühling nächsten Jahres fliege ich nach Europa. / In the spring of next year I'll fly to Europe.
Im Sommer ist es sehr heiß in New York. / In the summer it is very hot in New York.
Der Herbst ist die schönste Jahreszeit im Westen der Vereinigten Staaten. / Fall is the most beautiful season in the western United States.

16.4
RELATED
EXPRESSIONS

> **Days**
>
> *am Tag darauf* / the day after
> *den ganzen Tag* / all day long
> *gestern abend* / last night
> *vorgestern* / the day before yesterday
> *übermorgen* / the day after tomorrow

EXAMPLES:
Er arbeitete den ganzen Tag. / He worked all day long.
Übermorgen bin ich in Wien. / The day after tomorrow I'll be in Vienna.

> **MONTHS**
>
> *alle paar Monate* / every few months
> *Ende des Monats* / at the end of the month
> *vorigen Monat* / last month

EXAMPLES:

Wir besuchen ihn alle paar Monate. / We visit him every few months.

Ende des Monats haben wir meistens kein Geld. / At the end of the month we usually don't have any money.

Vorigen Monat war ich sehr beschäftigt. / Last month I was very busy.

Miscellaneous
auf Jahre hinaus / for years to come *bis auf weiteres* / for the present *bis vor kurzem* / until recently *im Handumdrehen* / in no time *über kurz oder lang* / sooner or later *vorläufig* / for the time being

EXAMPLES:

Bis auf weiteres brauche ich nichts. / For the present I do not need anything.

Er macht das im Handumdrehen. / He does it in no time.

Vorläufig bin ich zufrieden. / For the time being, I am satisfied.

§16.5
DATES

For dates use the ordinal numbers, followed by the month and the year.

EXAMPLES:

3. Juni 1986 (der dritte Juni [am dritten Juni] neunzehnhundert sechsundachtzig) / June 3, 1986

Welches Datum ist heute? / What's the date today?

Heute ist der achtzehnte November. / Today is the eighteenth of November.

Er fährt am ersten Juli weg. / He will leave on July first.

• Dates in a letter may be written in several ways:

Bonn, am 15. August 1986

OR

Bonn, den 15. August 1986

OR

Bonn, 15.8.1986 / Bonn, August 15, 1986

Note that in German the day precedes the month.

6

- Roman numerals are sometimes used in designating the month, mainly in business correspondence.

  EXAMPLE:

  Ich bestätige hiermit den Erhalt Ihres Schreibens vom 14. 3. 86 (14. III. 86) / I confirm herewith the receipt of your letter of March 14, 1986.

- Years are usually preceded by the words *im Jahre* (in the year), but *im Jahre* can be omitted.

  EXAMPLES:

  Er wurde im Jahre 1950 geboren.

  OR

  Er wurde 1950 geboren. / He was born in 1950.
  Kolumbus entdeckte Amerika 1492.

  OR

  Kolumbus entdeckte Amerika im Jahre 1492. / Columbus discovered America in 1492.

§16.6
THE WEATHER

Wie ist das Wetter? / How's the weather?
Könnte nicht besser sein. / Couldn't be better.
Es ist wunderbar. / It's wonderful.
Es ist miserabel. / It's miserable.
Es regnet Bindfäden. / It's raining cats and dogs.
Es donnert und blitzt. / There's thunder and lightning.
Es ist wahnsinnig heiß. / It is terribly hot.
Es ist eine Bärenkälte. / It is dreadfully cold.
Heute hat es gehagelt. / It hailed today.
Morgen wird es schneien. / It will snow tomorrow.

Der Wetterbericht / The weather forecast
die Temperatur / temperature
die Bewölkung / cloudiness
die Feuchtigkeit / humidity
der Niederschlag / precipitation
der Wolkenbruch / cloudburst
der Schneesturm / blizzard, snowstorm
das Hochdruckgebiet / high-pressure area

EXAMPLES:

Der Himmel ist teilweise bewölkt. / The sky is partly cloudy.

Die Feuchtigkeit liegt über dem Durchschnitt. / The humidity is above average.

Der Schneesturm über Bayern dauert schon drei Tage. / The blizzard over Bavaria is in its third day.

Über dem Rheinland ist ein Hochdruckgebiet. / There is a high-pressure area over the Rhineland.

Im Osten/Westen/Norden/Süden kommt es im Laufe des Tages zu sonnigen Abschnitten. / In the course of the day sunny periods will develop in the east/west/north/ south.

Regenwolken erstrecken sich von den Alpen bis zur Nordsee. / Rain clouds extend from the Alps to the North Sea.

§17.

Synonyms and Antonyms

Synonyms are words having the same or nearly the same meaning. They allow you to say the same thing in a slightly different way.

English Word(s)	German Synonyms
to admire	*bewundern, verehren, hochschätzen*
again	*wieder, nochmals, von neuem*
to aid	*helfen, unterstützen, beistehen*
although	*obwohl, obgleich, obschon*
angry	*ungehalten, aufgebracht, böse*
to answer	*antworten, erwidern, entgegnen*
anxious	*ängstlich, besorgt, bekümmert*
brave	*tapfer, mutig, unerschrocken*
complete	*komplett, vollkommen, ganz*
cosy	*behaglich, gemütlich, bequem*
customary	*gebräuchlich, herkömmlich, üblich*
delightful	*entzückend, köstlich, reizend*
to demand	*verlangen, fordern, begehren*
foolish	*dumm, albern, närrisch*
to happen	*geschehen, passieren, sich ereignen*
hideous	*entsetzlich, abscheulich, furchtbar*
hilarious	*vergnügt, heiter, ausgelassen*
honest	*ehrlich, redlich, rechtschaffen*
to intend	*beabsichtigen, vorhaben, bezwecken*
to investigate	*untersuchen, erforschen, ergründen*
kind	*freundlich, liebenswürdig, gütig*
label	*der Zettel, die Aufschrift, das Etikett*
misery	*das Elend, die Not, der Jammer*
nasty	*ekelhaft, widerlich, garstig*
now	*jetzt, nun, gegenwärtig*
to observe	*beobachten, wahrnehmen, bemerken*
obvious	*offensichtlich, offenkundig, handgreiflich*
odd	*sonderbar, seltsam, merkwürdig*
pain	*der Schmerz, der Kummer, die Pein*
to permit	*erlauben, gestatten, zulassen*
pleasant	*angenehm, wohltuend, erfreulich*
probably	*wahrscheinlich, vermutlich, mutmaßlich*
really	*wirklich, tatsächlich, eigentlich*
sad	*traurig, betrübt, niedergeschlagen*
spacious	*geräumig, weit, umfangreich*
stubborn	*hartnäckig, eigensinnig, starrköpfig*
sufficient	*genügend, hinlänglich, ausreichend*
talkative	*gesprächig, geschwätzig, redselig*
to teach	*lehren, unterrichten, beibringen*
trouble	*die Mühe, die Plage, die Störung*
wholesome	*zuträglich, heilsam, bekömmlich*

- The verbs *wissen* and *kennen* both mean "to know," but they are used in different ways.
- *Wissen* means to know something for a fact.

  EXAMPLES:
  Ich weiß, daß er reich ist. / I know that he is rich.
  Ich weiß, wo er wohnt. / I know where he lives.

- *Kennen* means to know in the sense of "to be acquainted with"; it refers to a person, place, or thing.

  EXAMPLES:
  Er kennt Herrn Müller. / He knows Mr. Müller.
  Sie kennt Wien. / She knows Vienna.

§17.2 ANTONYMS

Antonyms are words of opposite meaning.

alles / all	*nichts* / nothing
alt / old	*neu* / new
anfangen / to start	*aufhören* / to finish
arm / poor	*reich* / rich
der Beginn / the start	*das Ende* / the finish
bejahen / to affirm	*verneinen* / to deny
billig / cheap	*teuer* / expensive
damals / then	*jetzt* / now
erinnern / to remember	*vergessen* / to forget
erlauben / to allow	*verbieten* / to forbid
fest / solid	*flüssig* / liquid
finden / to find	*verlieren* / to lose
fleißig / industrious	*faul* / lazy
die Frage / question	*die Antwort* / answer
früh / early	*spät* / late
gesund / healthy	*krank* / ill
groß / big	*klein* / little
gut / good	*schlecht* / bad
hart / hard	*weich* / soft
jung / young	*alt* / old
der Krieg / war	*der Friede(n)* / peace
lachen / to laugh	*weinen* / to cry
langsam / slow	*schnell* / fast
leer / empty	*voll* / full
der Morgen / morning	*der Abend* / evening
sauber / clean	*schmutzig* / dirty
die Stadt / city	*das Land* / country
der Tag / day	*die Nacht* / night
viel / much	*wenig* / little
wild / wild	*zahm* / tame

VERB CHARTS

In the following charts you will find fully conjugated forms of some of the more representative German verbs. Their individual conjugations are displayed from left to right.

EXAMPLE:

kaufen in the present indicative:
ich kaufe (1st person singular), *du kaufst* (2nd person singular), *er kauft* (3rd person singular), *wir kaufen* (1st person plural), *ihr kauft* (2nd person plural), *sie kaufen* (3rd person plural)

aufen
buy

Present Indicative:	*ich kaufe, du kaufst, er kauft, wir kaufen, ihr kauft, sie kaufen*
Past:	*ich kaufte, du kauftest, er kaufte, wir kauften, ihr kauftet, sie kauften*
Present Perfect:	*ich habe gekauft, du hast gekauft, er hat gekauft, wir haben gekauft, ihr habt gekauft, sie haben gekauft*
Past Perfect:	*ich hatte gekauft, du hattest gekauft, er hatte gekauft, wir hatten gekauft, ihr hattet gekauft, sie hatten gekauft*
Future:	*ich werde kaufen, du wirst kaufen, er wird kaufen, wir werden kaufen, ihr werdet kaufen, sie werden kaufen*
Future Perfect:	*ich werde gekauft haben, du wirst gekauft haben, er wird gekauft haben, wir werden gekauft haben, ihr werdet gekauft haben, sie werden gekauft haben*
Imperative:	*kauf, kauft, kaufen Sie*
Present Subjunctive: (same as past tense)	
Past Subjunctive:	*ich hätte gekauft, du hättest gekauft, er hätte gekauft, wir hätten gekauft, ihr hättet gekauft, sie hätten gekauft*
Present Conditional:	*ich würde kaufen, du würdest kaufen, er würde kaufen, wir würden kaufen, ihr würdet kaufen, sie würden kaufen*

161

	Past Conditional:	*ich würde gekauft haben, du würdest gekauft haben, er würde gekauft haben, wir wür den gekauft haben, ihr würde gekauft haben, sie würden gekauft haben*
	Present Passive:	*es wird gekauft, sie werden gekauft*
	Past Passive:	*es wurde gekauft, sie wurden gekauft*
	Present Perfect Passive:	*es ist gekauft worden, sie sind gekauft worden*
	Future Passive:	*es wird gekauft werden, sie werden gekauft werden*

sich setzen **to sit down**	Present Indicative:	*ich setze mich, du setzt dich, er setzt sich, wir setzen uns, ihr setzt euch, sie setzen sich*
	Past:	*ich setzte mich, du setztest dich er setzte sich, wir setzten uns ihr setztet euch, sie setzten sic*
	Present Perfect:	*ich habe mich gesetzt, du hast dich gesetzt, er hat sich gesetzt, wir haben uns gesetz ihr habt euch gesetzt, sie haben sich gesetzt*
	Past Perfect:	*ich hatte mich gesetzt, du hatte dich gesetzt, er hatte sich gesetzt, wir hatten uns gesetz ihr hattet euch gesetzt, sie hatten sich gesetzt*
	Future:	*ich werde mich setzen, du wirst dich setzen, er wird sich setzen, wir werden uns setzen, ihr werdet euch setzen, sie werden sich setze*
	Future Perfect:	*ich werde mich gesetzt haben, du wirst dich gesetzt haben, er wird sich gesetzt haben, wir werden uns gesetzt haben, ih werdet euch gesetzt haben, sie werden sich gesetzt habe*
	Imperative:	*setz dich, setzt euch, setzen Sie sich*

Present Subjunctive: (same as past tense)

Past Subjunctive:	*ich hätte mich gesetzt, du hättest dich gesetzt, er hätte sich gesetzt, wir hätten uns gesetzt, ihr hättet euch gesetzt, sie hätten sich gesetzt*
Present Conditional:	*ich würde mich setzen, du würdest dich setzen, er würde sich setzen, wir würden uns setzen, ihr würdet euch setzen, sie würden sich setzen*
Past Conditional:	*ich würde mich gesetzt haben, du würdest dich gesetzt haben, er würde sich gesetzt haben, wir würden uns gesetzt haben, ihr würdet euch gesetzt haben, sie würden sich gesetzt haben*

leiben
o remain

Present Indicative:	*ich bleibe, du bleibst, er bleibt, wir bleiben, ihr bleibt, sie bleiben*
Past:	*ich blieb, du bliebst, er blieb, wir blieben, ihr bliebt, sie blieben*
Present Perfect:	*ich bin geblieben, du bist geblieben, er ist geblieben, wir sind geblieben, ihr seid geblieben, sie sind geblieben*
Past Perfect:	*ich war geblieben, du warst geblieben, er war geblieben, wir waren geblieben, ihr wart geblieben, sie waren geblieben*
Future:	*ich werde bleiben, du wirst bleiben, er wird bleiben, wir werden bleiben, ihr werdet bleiben, sie werden bleiben*
Future Perfect:	*ich werde geblieben sein, du wirst geblieben sein, er wird geblieben sein, wir werden geblieben sein, ihr werdet geblieben sein, sie werden geblieben sein*
Imperative:	*bleib, bleibt, bleiben Sie*

Present Subjunctive:	*ich bliebe, du bliebest, er bliebe, wir blieben, ihr bliebet, sie blieben*
Past Subjunctive:	*ich wäre geblieben, du wärest geblieben, er wäre geblieben, wir wären geblieben, ihr wäre geblieben, sie wären gebliebe*
Present Conditional:	*ich würde bleiben, du würdest bleiben, er würde bleiben, wir würden bleiben, ihr würdet bleiben, sie würden bleiben*
Past Conditional:	*ich würde geblieben sein, du würdest geblieben sein, er würde geblieben sein, wir wür den geblieben sein, ihr würde geblieben sein, sie würden geblieben sein*

fallen
to fall

Present Indicative:	*ich falle, du fällst, er fällt, wir fallen, ihr fallt, sie fallen*
Past:	*ich fiel, du fielst, er fiel, wir fielen, ihr fielt, sie fielen*
Present Perfect:	*ich bin gefallen, du bist gefallen, er ist gefallen, wir sind gefal-len, ihr seid gefallen, sie sind gefallen*
Past Perfect:	*ich war gefallen, etc.*
Future:	*ich werde fallen, etc.*
Future Perfect:	*ich werde gefallen sein, etc.*
Imperative:	*fall, fallt, fallen Sie*
Present Subjunctive:	*ich fiele, du fielest, er fiele, wir fielen, ihr fielet, sie fielen*
Past Subjunctive:	*ich wäre gefallen, du wärest gefallen, er wäre gefallen, wir wären gefallen, ihr wäret gefallen, sie wären gefallen*
Present Conditional:	*ich würde fallen, etc.*
Past Conditional:	*ich würde gefallen sein, etc.*

kommen
to come

Present Indicative:	*ich komme, du kommst, er kommt, wir kommen, ihr kommt, sie kommen*
Past:	*ich kam, du kamst, er kam, wir kamen, ihr kamt, sie kamen*

Present Perfect:	*ich bin gekommen, du bist gekommen, er ist gekommen, wir sind gekommen, ihr seid gekommen, sie sind gekommen*
Past Perfect:	*ich war gekommen,* etc.
Future:	*ich werde kommen,* etc.
Future Perfect:	*ich werde gekommen sein,* etc.
Imperative:	*komm, kommt, kommen Sie*
Present Subjunctive:	*ich käme, du kämest, er käme, wir kämen, ihr kämet, sie kämen*
Past Subjunctive:	*ich wäre gekommen, du wärest gekommen, er wäre gekommen, wir wären gekommen, ihr wäret gekommen, sie wären gekommen*
Present Conditional:	*ich würde kommen,* etc.
Past Conditional:	*ich würde gekommen sein,* etc.

esen
o read

Present Indicative:	*ich lese, du liest, er liest, wir lesen, ihr lest, sie lesen*
Past:	*ich las, du last, er las, wir lasen, ihr last, sie lasen*
Present Perfect:	*ich habe gelesen, du hast gelesen, er hat gelesen, wir haben gelesen, ihr habt gelesen, sie haben gelesen*
Past Perfect:	*ich hatte gelesen, du hattest gelesen, er hatte gelesen, wir hatten gelesen, ihr hattest gelesen, sie hatten gelesen*
Future:	*ich werde lesen,* etc.
Future Perfect:	*ich werde gelesen haben,* etc.
Imperative:	*lies, lest, lesen Sie*
Present Subjunctive:	*ich läse, du läsest, er läse, wir läsen, ihr läset, sie läsen*
Past Subjunctive:	*ich hätte gelesen, du hättest gelesen, er hätte gelesen, wir hätten gelesen, ihr hättet gelesen, sie hätten gelesen*
Present Conditional:	*ich würde lesen,* etc.
Past Conditional:	*ich würde gelesen haben,* etc.
Present Passive:	*es wird gelesen, sie werden gelesen*
Past Passive:	*es wurde gelesen, sie wurden gelesen*

	Present Perfect Passive:	*es ist gelesen worden, sie sind gelesen worden*
	Future Passive:	*es wird gelesen werden, sie werden gelesen werden*
sehen **to see**	Present Indicative:	*ich sehe, du siehst, er sieht, wir sehen, ihr seht, sie sehen*
	Past:	*ich sah, du sahst, er sah, wir sahen, ihr saht, sie sahen*
	Present Perfect:	*ich habe gesehen, du hast gesehen, er hat gesehen, wir haben gesehen, ihr habt gesehen, sie haben gesehen*
	Past Perfect:	*ich hatte gesehen,* etc.
	Future:	*ich werde sehen,* etc.
	Future Perfect:	*ich werde gesehen haben,* etc.
	Imperative:	*sieh, seht, sehen Sie*
	Present Subjunctive:	*ich sähe, du sähest, er sähe, wir sähen, ihr sähet, sie sähen*
	Past Subjunctive:	*ich hätte gesehen, du hättest gesehen, er hätte gesehen, wir hätten gesehen, ihr hättet gesehen, sie hätten gesehen*
	Present Conditional:	*ich würde sehen,* etc.
	Past Conditional:	*ich würde gesehen haben,* etc.
	Present Passive:	*ich werde gesehen, du wirst gesehen, er wird gesehen, wir werden gesehen, ihr werdet gesehen, sie werden gesehen*
	Past Passive:	*ich wurde gesehen, du wurdest gesehen, er wurde gesehen, wir wurden gesehen, ihr wurdet gesehen, sie wurden gesehen*
	Present Perfect Passive:	*ich bin gesehen worden, du bist gesehen worden, er ist gesehen worden, wir sind gesehen worden, ihr seid gesehen worden, sie sind gesehen worden*
	Future Passive:	*ich werde gesehen werden, du wirst gesehen werden, er wird gesehen werden, wir werden gesehen werden, ihr werdet gesehen werden, sie werden gesehen werden*

sitzen
o sit

Present Indicative:	*ich sitze, du sitzt, er sitzt, wir sitzen, ihr sitzt, sie sitzen*
Past:	*ich saß, du saßest, er saß, wir saßen, ihr saßest, sie saßen*
Present Perfect:	*ich habe gesessen, du hast gesessen, er hat gesessen, wir haben gesessen, ihr habt gesessen, sie haben gesessen*
Past Perfect:	*ich hatte gesessen,* etc.
Future:	*ich werde sitzen,* etc.
Future Perfect:	*ich werde gesessen haben,* etc.
Imperative:	*sitz, sitzt, sitzen Sie*
Present Subjunctive:	*ich säße, du säßest, er säße, wir säßen, ihr säßet, sie säßen*
Past Subjunctive:	*ich hätte gesessen, du hättest gesessen, er hätte gesessen, wir hätten gesessen, ihr hättet gesessen, sie hätten gesessen*
Present Conditional:	*ich würde sitzen,* etc.
Past Conditional:	*ich würde gesessen haben,* etc.

sprechen
o speak

Present Indicative:	*ich spreche, du sprichst, er spricht, wir sprechen, ihr sprecht, sie sprechen*
Past:	*ich sprach, du sprachst, er sprach, wir sprachen, ihr spracht, sie sprachen*
Present Perfect:	*ich habe gesprochen, du hast gesprochen, er hat gesprochen, wir haben gesprochen, ihr habt gesprochen, sie haben gesprochen*
Past Perfect:	*ich hatte gesprochen,* etc.
Future:	*ich werde sprechen,* etc.
Future Perfect:	*ich werde gesprochen haben,* etc.
Imperative:	*sprich, sprecht, sprechen Sie*
Present Subjunctive:	*ich spräche, du sprächest, er spräche, wir sprächen, ihr sprächet, sie sprächen*
Past Subjunctive:	*ich hätte gesprochen, du hättest gesprochen, er hätte gesprochen, wir hätten gesprochen, ihr hättet gesprochen, sie hätten gesprochen*
Present Conditional:	*ich würde sprechen,* etc.
Past Conditional:	*ich würde gesprochen haben,* etc.

stehen
to stand

Present Indicative:	*ich stehe, du stehst, er steht, wi stehen, ihr steht, sie stehen*
Past:	*ich stand, du stand(e)st, er stand, wir standen, ihr standet, sie standen*
Present Perfect:	*ich habe gestanden, du hast gestanden, er hat gestanden, wi haben gestanden, ihr habt gestanden, sie haben gestander*
Past Perfect:	*ich hatte gestanden, etc.*
Future:	*ich werde stehen, etc.*
Future Perfect:	*ich werde gestanden haben, etc*
Imperative:	*steh, steht, stehen Sie*
Present Subjunctive:	*ich stünde, du stündest, er stünde, wir stünden, ihr stündet, sie stünden*
Past Subjunctive:	*ich hätte gestanden, du hättest gestanden, er hätte gestanden, wir hätten gestanden, ihr hättet gestanden, sie hätten gestander*
Present Conditional:	*ich würde stehen, etc.*
Past Conditional:	*ich würde gestanden haben, etc*

es können
to know it, to be able to do it

Present Indicative:	*ich kann es, du kannst es, er kann es, wir können es, ihr könr es, sie können es*
Past:	*ich konnte es, du konntest es, er konnte es, wir konnten es, ihr konntet es, sie konnten es*
Present Perfect:	*ich habe es gekonnt, du hast es gekonnt, er hat es gekonnt, wir haben es gekonnt, ihr habt es gekonnt, sie haben es gekonnt*
Past Perfect:	*ich hatte es gekonnt, etc.*
Future:	*ich werde es können, du wirst e können, er wird es können, wir werden es können, ihr werdet es können, sie werden es können*
Future Perfect:	*ich werde es gekonnt haben, etc*
Present Subjunctive:	*ich könnte es, du könntest es, er könnte es, wir könnten es, ihr könntet es, sie könnten es*
Past Subjunctive:	*ich hätte es gekonnt, du hättest es gekonnt, er hätte es gekonnt, wir hätten es gekonnt, ihr hättet es gekonnt, sie hätten es gekonr*

Present Conditional: *ich würde es können, du würdest es können, er würde es können, wir würden es können, ihr würdet es können, sie würden es können*

Past Conditional: *ich würde es gekonnt haben, du würdest es gekonnt haben, er würde es gekonnt haben, wir würden es gekonnt haben, ihr würdet es gekonnt haben, sie würden es gekonnt haben*

s lesen können
b be able to read it

Present Indicative: *ich kann es lesen, du kannst es lesen, er kann es lesen, wir können es lesen, ihr könnt es lesen, sie können es lesen*

Past: *ich konnte es lesen, du konntest es lesen, er konnte es lesen, wir konnten es lesen, ihr konntet es lesen, sie konnten es lesen*

Present Perfect: *ich habe es lesen können, du hast es lesen können, er hat es lesen können, wir haben es lesen können, ihr habt es lesen kön-nen, sie haben es lesen können*

Past Perfect: *ich hatte es lesen können, etc.*

Future: *ich werde es lesen können, etc.*

Subjunctive: *ich hätte es lesen können, du hättest es lesen können, er hätte es lesen können, wir hätten es lesen können, ihr hättet es lesen können, sie hätten es lesen können*

Conditional: *ich würde es lesen können, du würdest es lesen können, er würde es lesen können, wir wür-den es lesen können, ihr würdet es lesen können, sie würden es lesen können*

Common Strong and Irregular Verbs

Infinitive	Present Indicative	Past Tense	Past Participle		Meaning
backen	bäckt	backte (buk)		gebacken	to bake
befehlen	befehlt	befahl		befohlen	to order
beginnen	beginnt	begann		begonnen	to begin
beißen	beißt	biß		gebissen	to bite
biegen	biegt	bog		gebogen	to bend
bieten	bietet	bot		geboten	to offer
binden	bindet	band		gebunden	to bind
bitten	bittet	bat		gebeten	to ask
blasen	bläst	blies		geblasen	to blow
bleiben	bleibt	blieb	ist	geblieben	to stay
braten	brät	briet		gebraten	to roast
brechen	bricht	brach		gebrochen	to break
brennen	brennt	brannte		gebrannt	to burn
bringen	bringt	brachte		gebracht	to bring
denken	denkt	dachte		gedacht	to think
dürfen	darf	durfte		gedurft dürfen	to be permitted (may)
empfehlen	empfielt	empfahl		empfohlen	to recommend
essen	ißt	aß		gegessen	to eat
fahren	fährt	fuhr	ist	gefahren	to travel
fallen	fällt	fiel	ist	gefallen	to fall
fangen	fängt	fing		gefangen	to catch
finden	findet	fand		gefunden	to find
fliegen	fliegt	flog	ist	geflogen	to fly
fliehen	flieht	floh	ist	geflohen	to flee
fließen	fließt	floß	ist	geflossen	to flee
frieren	friert	fror		gefroren	to freeze
gären	gärt	gor		gegoren	to ferment
geben	gibt	gab		gegeben	to give
gehen	geht	ging	ist	gegangen	to go
gelingen	gelingt	gelang	ist	gelungen	to succeed
geschehen	geschieht	geschah	ist	geschehen	to happen
gewinnen	gewinnt	gewann		gewonnen	to win
gießen	gießt	goß		gegossen	to pour
graben	gräbt	grub		gegraben	to dig
greifen	greift	griff		gegriffen	to seize
haben	hat	hatte		gehabt	to have
halten	hält	hielt		gehalten	to hold
hauen	haut	hieb		gehauen	to hit, to beat
heben	hebt	hob		gehoben	to lift
heißen	heißt	hieß		geheißen	to call
helfen	hilft	half		geholfen	to help
kennen	kennt	kannte		gekannt	to know
klingen	klingt	klang		geklungen	to sound
kommen	kommt	kam	ist	gekommen	to come
können	kann	konnte		gekonnt können	to be able to (could)
kriechen	kriecht	kroch	ist	gekrochen	to crawl
laden	lädt	lud		geladen	to load

finitive	Present Indicative	Past Tense	Past Participle	Meaning
ssen	läßt	ließ	gelassen lassen	to let
ufen	läuft	lief	ist gelaufen	to run
iden	leidet	litt	gelitten	to suffer
ihen	leiht	lieh	geliehen	to lend
sen	liest	las	gelesen	to read
egen	liegt	lag	gelegen	to lie
gen	lügt	log	gelogen	to lie
eiden	meidet	mied	gemieden	to avoid
essen	mißt	maß	gemessen	to measure
ißlingen	mißlingt	mißlang	ist mißlungen	to fail
ögen	mag	mochte	gemocht mögen	to like to (may)
üssen	muß	mußte	gemußt müssen	to have to (must)
ehmen	nimmt	nahm	genommen	to take
ennen	nennt	nannte	genannt	to name
feifen	pfeift	pfiff	gepfiffen	to whistle
aten	rät	riet	geraten	to advise
eißen	reißt	riß	gerissen	to tear
eiten	reitet	ritt	ist geritten	to ride
ennen	rennt	rannte	ist gerannt	to run
echen	riecht	roch	gerochen	to smell
ufen	ruft	rief	gerufen	to call
chaffen	schafft	schuf	geschaffen	to create
cheinen	scheint	schien	geschienen	to shine, to seem
cheren	schert	schor	geschoren	to shear
chießen	schießt	schoß	geschossen	to shoot
chlafen	schläft	schlief	geschlaffen	to sleep
chlagen	schlägt	schlug	geschlagen	to beat
chließen	schließt	schloß	geschlossen	to close
chneiden	schneidet	schnitt	geschnitten	to cut
chreiben	schreibt	schrieb	geschrieben	to write
chreien	schreit	schrie	geschrie(e)n	to cry (out)
chweigen	schweigt	schwiegt	geschwiegen	to be silent
chwimmen	schwimmt	schwamm	ist geschwommen	to swim
chwingen	schwingt	schwang	geschwungen	to swing
chwören	schwört	schwor	geschworen	to swear
ehen	sieht	sah	gesehen	to see
ein	ist	war	ist gewesen	to be
enden	sendet	sandte	gesandt	to send
ingen	singt	sang	gesungen	to sing
inken	sinkt	sank	ist gesunken	to sink
itzen	sitzt	saß	gesessen	to sit
ollen	soll	sollte	gesollt, sollen	to be supposed to (schould)
pinnen	spinnt	spann	gesponnen	to spin
prechen	spricht	sprach	gesprochen	to speak
pringen	springt	sprang	ist gesprungen	to jump
techen	sticht	stach	gestochen	to sting, to jab
tecken	steckt	stak	gesteckt	to stick
tehen	steht	stand	gestanden	to stand

Infinitive	Present Indicative	Past Tense	Past Participle		Meaning
stehlen	stiehlt	stahl		gestohlen	to steal
steigen	steigt	stieg	ist	gestiegen	to go up
sterben	stirbt	starb	ist	gestorben	to die
stinken	stinkt	stank		gestunken	to stink
stoßen	stößt	stieß		gestoßen	to push
streichen	streicht	strich		gestrichen	to stroke
streiten	streitet	stritt		gestritten	to quarrel
tragen	trägt	trug		getragen	to carry, to wear
treffen	trifft	traf		getroffen	to meet
treten	tritt	trat	ist	getreten	to step
trinken	trinkt	trank		getrunken	to drink
tun	tut	tat		getan	to do
verbergen	verbirgt	verbarg		verborgen	to hide
verderben	verdirbt	verdarb		verdorben	to spoil
vergessen	vergißt	vergaß		vergessen	to forget
vergleichen	vergleicht	verglich		verglichen	to compare
verlieren	verliert	verlor		verloren	to lose
verzeihen	verzeiht	verzieh		verziehen	to forgive
wachsen	wächst	wuchs	ist	gewachen	to grow
waschen	wäscht	wusch		gewaschen	to wash
weben	webt	wob		gewoben	to weave
wenden	wendet	wandte		gewandt	to turn
werden	wird	wurde	ist	geworden	to become
werfen	wirft	warf		geworfen	to throw
wissen	weiß	wußte		gewußt	to know
wollen	will	wollte		gewollt wollen	to want to
zerreißen	zerreißt	zerriß		zerrissen	to tear apart
ziehen	zieht	zog		gezogen	to draw, pull
zwingen	zwingt	zwang		gezwungen	to force

Note: Present indicative and past-tense verbs are given in the third person singular.

LET'S REVIEW

Test Yourself

1. The *w* in *schwimmen* is pronounced like the first letter of
   - wisdom ☐
   - whether ☐
   - vain ☐

2. The *z* in *zehn* is similar to the sound in
   - zip ☐
   - tsar ☐
   - silk ☐

3. The word *mein* rhymes with
   - keen ☐
   - mean ☐
   - fine ☐

4. The *u* in *Uhr* is like the sound in
   - lure ☐
   - unit ☐
   - unload ☐

5. The *eu* in *heute* is similar to the sound in
   - road ☐
   - boy ☐
   - Hugh ☐

6. The *st* in *Stadt* sounds like
   - *sht* ☐
   - *st* ☐
   - *ts* ☐

7. The *chs* in *Büchse* (box) sounds like
   - *sh* ☐
   - *gs* ☐
   - *ks* ☐

8. The *eh* in *fehlt* rhymes with
   - mailed ☐
   - field ☐
   - held ☐

9. The *au* in *glaube* is similar to the vowel sound in
   - mouse ☐
   - taught ☐
   - food ☐

10. The *y* in *Zypern* (Cyprus) is pronounced like

ü ☐
i ☐
u ☐

In the following words, underline the stressed syllable.

11. der Gartenstuhl (garden chair), gegangen (gone), stu dieren (to study), die Brauerei (brewery)

§2. ORTHOG-RAPHY

Underline the words that should be capitalized:

12. freundlich, freund, zeit, neu, nase, die neun, das schwimmen, der amerikanische präsident

Underline the phrases that are spelled correctly.

13. *das Alte* (the old one), *etwas Kleines* (something little *viel nettes* (much that is nice)

How would you divide the word *Ansichtskarte* (picture postcard) at the end of the line?

14.
Ansichts-karte ☐
Ansicht-skarte ☐
Ansic-htskarte ☐

How would you divide the word *Bäcker* (baker)?

15.
Bäk-ker ☐
Bäck-er ☐
Bä-cker ☐

How would you write "Queen Elizabeth II" in German?

16.
Königin Elizabeth II. ☐
Königin Elizabeth II ☐

In the following sentences the commas have been omitted Can you put them where they belong?

17. Fritz trank Kaffee und Edith trank Tee.

18. Er glaubt daß du recht hast.

19. Wenn du zurückkommst gehen wir ins Kino.

20. Ich weiß nicht ob ich das tun kann.

21. Ich reise nach Italien Spanien und Frankreich.

22. Er kaufte sich ein Hemd einen Schlips und Schuhe.

Choose the expression below that should *not* have an exclamation mark.

23.   *Ich werde heute ins Kino gehen!* □
      Eingang verboten!   □
      Liebe Anna!   □

3.
WORD ORDER

In the following sentences the words are scrambled. Rearrange them correctly to form sentences, starting with the subject.

24. mit ihr / Karl / im Wohnzimmer / arbeitet _____

25. dem Mädchen / die Geschichte / er / erzählt _____

26. ins Büro / Paul / vor einer Stunde / ging _____

Rearrange the words in the sentences below, starting with the adverb.

27. wir / aus / gehen / natürlich _____

28. er / zurück / gestern / kam _____

29. fährt / mit / morgen / er _____

Rearrange the words below, starting with the object.

30. will / ihrem Bruder / helfen / sie _____

31. sehen / ich / werde / den Vater _____

32. ich / auf ihn / warten / mußte _____

In the sentence pairs below, underline the sentence with the correct word order.

33. Ich gebe ein Buch dem Vater.
 Ich gebe dem Vater ein Buch.

34. Ich kaufe der Tante ein Geschenk.
 Ich kaufe ein Geschenk der Tante.

In the pairs of negative sentences below, which sentence has the correct word order?

35. Er hat heute studiert nicht.
 Er hat heute nicht studiert.

36. Fritz arbeitete nicht leider heute.
 Fritz arbeitete heute leider nicht.

37. Nicht sie, sondern er spielt heute Bridge.
 Sie nicht, sondern er spielt heute Bridge.

Rearrange the words in the sentences below to form questions. (Start with the interrogative.)

38. die Tür / warum / öffnen / Sie _____

39. das Sofa / gekostet / hat / wieviel _____

40. kommt / wann / er _____

Below are pairs of complex sentences. Underline the sentence with the correct word order.

41. Das Mädchen, das wirft (throws) den Ball, ist meine Schwester.
    Das Mädchen, das den Ball wirft, ist meine Schweste

42. Bevor du ins Kino gehst, mußt du mir helfen.
    Bevor du gehst ins Kino, du mußt mir helfen.

43. Weil ich kein Geld habe, ich kann nichts kaufen.
    Weil ich kein Geld habe, kann ich nichts kaufen.

44. Ich lese weniger, seit du hier bist.
    Ich lese weniger, seit du bist hier.

§4. NOUNS

In the sentences below, fill in the definite articles (der, die, das) to give the correct gender of the nouns

45. _____ Kind ist zu Hause.

46. _____ Eiche ist ein Baum.

47. _____ Wasser ist kalt.

48. _____ Schlips ist rot.

49. _____ Garage ist um die Ecke.

50. _____ Klima ist sehr gut.

51. _____ Iran ist in Asien.

52. _____ Instrument ist teuer.

53. _____ Kunde kauft ein Buch.

54. _____ Zahnbürste ist neu.

Fill in the correct definite articles for the following noncou nouns.

55. _____ Salz, _____ Hunger, _____ Ferien, _____ Ge-sundheit, _____ Möbel

In the sentences below, fill in the correct German forms of the English nouns in parentheses.

EXAMPLE:
Das ist das Buch des _____ (father).
Das ist das Buch des <u>Vaters.</u>

56. Er gibt dem _____ Geld. (boy)

57. Sie telefoniert der _____ . (woman)

58. Hast du die Adresse des _____ ? (physician)

59. Wir nehmen das _____ mit. (child)

60. Er dankt dem _____ . (father)

Change the nouns in the singular to the plural by putting in the correct plural forms.

61. Ich kenne das Mädchen. Ich kenne die _____ .

62. Wo ist der Löffel? Wo sind die _____ ?

63. Der Apfel ist rot. Die _____ sind rot.

64. Ich danke dem Lehrer. Ich danke den _____ .

65. Er liest den Brief. Er liest die _____ .

66. Das Haus ist groß. Die _____ sind groß.

67. Sie wäscht das Glas. Sie wäscht die _____ .

68. Er hilft dem Mann. Er hilft den _____ .

69. Er liest die Zeitung. Er liest die _____ .

70. Die Tür ist offen. Die _____ sind offen.

71. Der Tee ist in der Tasse. Der Tee ist in den _____ .

72. Er repariert das Radio. Er repariert die _____ .

73. Man sitzt auf dem Sofa. Man sitzt auf den _____ .

Change the nouns below to the plural.

74. Der Name ist deutsch. Die _____ sind deutsch.

75. Das Herz ist ein Muskel. Die _____ sind Muskeln.

76. Was ist das Thema? Was sind die _____ ?

77. Ich kenne den Rhythmus. Ich kenne die _____ .

78. Wo ist das Museum? Wo sind die _____ ?

In the following puzzle there are four nouns with the plural ending -s. Try to find them.

79.

P	A	R	K	S	T	L	H	K
M	O	N	A	W	I	N	O	M
K	A	M	M	E	M	D	T	S
O	P	Z	E	R	D	T	E	R
A	L	G	R	O	N	A	L	A
G	B	Z	A	U	T	O	S	N
A	B	O	S	L	I	N	G	T

Fill in the correct forms of the Saxon genitive.

80. Das ist _____ Auto. (of the father)

81. Ich bin in _____ Hauptstadt. (of France)

82. Ich freue mich auf _____ Museen. (of London)

§5.
ARTICLES

In the sentence pairs below, underline the version showing the correct use of the definite article.

83. Der Tod ist unvermeidlich. (unavoidable)
    Tod ist unvermeidlich.

84. Natur ist sehr schön.
    Die Natur ist sehr schön.

85. Wir haben die Geduld.
    Wir haben Geduld.

86. Ätna ist in Sizilien.
    Der Ätna ist in Sizilien.

87. Heute ist der 5. April.
    Heute ist 5. April.

Underline the version showing the correct use of the indefinite article.

88. Ich bin Spanier.
    Ich bin ein Spanier.

89. Sie wird eine Lehrerin.
    Sie wird Lehrerin.

90. Wir fragten ihn als einen Fachmann. (expert)
    Wir fragten ihn als Fachmann.

91. Er hat Temperatur.
    Er hat eine Temperatur.

In the sentences below, fill in the correct forms of the demonstrative indicated by the English forms in parentheses.

EXAMPLES:
Siehst du _____, _____ *Mann? (this)*
Siehst du <u>den, diesen</u> *Mann?*

Ich spreche mit _____ *Frau (that, farther away).*
Ich spreche mit <u>jener</u> *Frau.*

92. _____, _____ Kleid ist sehr schön. (this)

93. Sie spricht mit _____, _____ Leuten. (these)

94. Er gibt es _____, _____ Jungen. (to this)

95. _____ ist ein neues Buch. (this)

96. _____ Leute sind sehr nett. (those, farther away)

In the following sentences the endings of the definite articles, indefinite articles, or demonstratives have been omitted. Fill in the correct endings.

97. Ich zeige es d ____ Studentin.

98. Er schreibt ein _____ Fräulein.

99. Hier ist das Bild d ____ Mannes.

100. Wir besuchen d ____ Schule.

101. Sie schickt es dies ____ Lehrer.

102. Er hat ein ____ Tochter.

103. Wir bringen es d ____ Söhnen.

104. Das gehört dies ____ Kindern.

105. Das ist die Tasche ein ____ Mädchens.

106. Kennen Sie den Namen dies ____ Lehrers?

**6.
DJECTIVES**

In the sentences below, fill in the blanks with the appropriate weak adjective endings.

107. Ich mag den gut ____ Jungen.

108. Die schön ____ Tochter wohnt hier.

109. Er dankt dem blond ____ Mädchen.

110. Das ist ein Bild jener alt ____ Frau.

111. Ich besuche das neu _____ Museum.

112. Er zeigt es den nett _____ Freunden.

113. Sie hilft dem klein _____ Kind.

114. Ich trage jedes neu _____ Kleid sofort.

115. Er liebt alle alt _____ Sachen.

Fill in the blanks with the appropriate strong adjective ending

116. Gut _____ Mann, dein Freund!

117. Schön _____ Mädchen, deine Tochter!

118. Das sind alt _____ Geschichten.

119. Wir haben ander _____ Sorgen.

120. Sie hat drei klein _____ Nichten.

121. Wir haben groß _____ Glück damit.

122. Frisch _____ Blumen riechen gut.

Fill in the blanks with the appropriate mixed adjective ending

123. Sie ist eine gut _____ Freundin.

124. Er kam mit einem neu _____ Anzug.

125. Sein alt _____ Radio ist kaputt.

126. Ich liebe unsere alt _____ Bäume.

127. Hier gibt es keine neu _____ Häuser.

The following sentences contain adjectives used as nouns
Fill in the appropriate endings.

128. Gibst du es der Klein _____?

129. Der Alt _____ war im Krankenhaus.

130. Diese Blond _____ ist sehr hübsch.

131. Er ist ein Bekannt _____ von uns.

132. Ich habe etwas Gut _____ für dich.

Fill in the appropriate comparative and superlative forms
the adjectives.

EXAMPLE:
Paul ist jung. Fred ist jünger. Bob ist der Jüngste. Bob ist am jüngsten.

133. Hans ist gesund. Karl ist _____. Peter ist der _____. Peter ist am _____.

134. Er ist arm. Sie ist _____. Wir sind die _____. Wir sind am _____.

135. Der Berg ist hoch. Dieser Berg ist _____. Jener Berg ist der _____. Jener Berg ist am _____.

136. Das Brot ist gut. Dieses Brot ist _____. Jenes Brot ist das _____. Jenes Brot ist am _____.

137. Eva hat viel. Grete hat _____. Karla hat am _____.

Make an appropriate comparison by filling in the missing word.

138. Sie ist so klug _____ ich.

139. Er ist schneller _____ du.

7.
PRONOUNS

Insert the missing subject pronouns.

140. Hans, _____ bist ein gutes Kind.

141. Fritz war in München. _____ spricht gut Deutsch.

142. Wo ist das Buch? Hier ist _____.

143. Herr Schmidt, kommen _____ mit uns?

144. Die Arbeit war schwer. _____ bin müde.

145. Karl und Franz, wo seid _____?

146. Du und ich, _____ gehen jetzt nach Hause.

147. Die Eltern sind nicht zu Hause. _____ sind in Italien.

148. Meine Damen, spielen _____ Bridge?

Insert the missing object pronouns in the accusative.

149. Siehst du Otto? Ja, ich sehe _____.

150. Kennt er meine Freundin? Ja, er kennt _____.

151. Macht Mutter das Frühstück? Ja, sie macht _____.

152. Triffst du mich heute? Ja, ich treffe _____.

153. Liebt er dich? Ja, er liebt _____.

154. Kauft ihr die Kleider? Ja, wir kaufen _____.

155. Kennst du Anny und mich? Ja, ich kenne _____.

156. Meint er euch damit? Ja, er meint _____.

157. Erinnern Sie sich an Paul und mich? Ja, ich erinnere mich an _____.

Insert the missing object pronouns in the dative.

158. Hilft er dir? Ja, er hilft _____.

159. Zeigt er mir das Auto? Ja, er zeigt es _____.

160. Gibst du Elsa das Buch? Ja, ich gebe es _____.

161. Kaufst du Franz die Uhr? Ja, ich kaufe sie _____

162. Erzählst du dem Kind eine Geschichte? Ja, ich erzähle sie _____.

163. Bringst du den Mädchen Bonbons? Ja, ich bringe _____ Bonbons.

164. Schickt er euch Karten? Ja, er schickt _____ Karten.

165. Kommt er heute zu uns? Ja, er kommt heute zu _____.

166. Haben Sie uns Blumen geschickt? Ja, ich habe _____ Blumen geschickt.

Insert the missing reflexive pronouns.

167. Ich lege _____ aufs Sofa.

168. Wir müssen _____ rasieren.

169. Erinnerst du _____?

170. Ich putze _____ die Schuhe.

171. Hast du _____ eine Zeitung gekauft?

172. Haben Sie _____ das Bier bestellt?

173. Sie schreiben _____. (to each other)

Insert the missing possessive adjectives.

174. _____ (his) Bruder ist sehr stark.

175. Er besucht _____ (our) Tante.

176. Hier ist _____ (your) Buch, Herr Schmidt.

177. Das ist das Bild _____ (of my) Freundes.

178. Fritz und Elsa, hier ist _____ (your, familiar) Geschenk.

179. Sie gibt es _____ (to her) Kind.

180. Wir verstehen _____ (your, formal) Sorgen. (worries)

Insert the missing possessive pronouns.

181. Ich habe meinen Bleistift. Hast du den _____? (yours)

182. Da steht ein Fahrrad. (bicycle). Ist es _____? (yours, familiar)

183. Sie ist _____ (his) und er ist _____. (yours, familiar)

Insert the missing relative pronouns.

184. Das ist der Mann, _____ du helfen willst.

185. Hier ist der Schlips, _____ du suchst.

186. Wer ist der Junge, _____ das geschrieben hat?

187. Kennst du das Fräulein, _____ dort sitzt?

188. Das Kleid, _____ du trägst, ist sehr hübsch.

189. Ist die Frau, mit _____ du telefonierst, deine Tante?

190. Wo ist der Junge, _____ Ball hier liegt?

191. Das sind die Leute, _____ Auto beschädigt wurde. (was damaged)

192. Hier sind die Bilder, _____ du magst.

193. Sind das die Personen, _____ du schreibst?

Make up appropriate questions to the following answers, using the forms of *wer* (who), *was* (what), and *welch-* (which).

EXAMPLE:
Er liest ein Buch. Was liest er?

194. Otto wohnt in München. (who) _____?

195. Das ist Karls Mantel. (whose) _____?

196. Der Ball gehört dem Kind. (to whom) _____?

197. Albert sieht seinen Bruder. (whom) _____?

198. Sie spielen Bridge. (what) _____?

199. Dieses Auto gefällt ihm. (which) _____?

200. Dieser Mann ist am größten. (which) _____?

Correct the following sentences by using combinations with
wo- or *wor-*.

201. An was arbeitet er? —————?

202. Von was redet sie? —————?

203. Über was lachst du? —————?

204. Für was braucht er es? —————?

Insert the German equivalents of the indefinite pronouns in
parentheses.

205. Heute kommt —————. (nobody)

206. Ich muß Ihnen ————— sagen. (something)

207. Morgen spielt ————— hier Hamlet. (one)

208. In dieser Schule lernt er —————. (nothing)

209. Sie kennt ————— Gefahren. (all)

Insert the correct forms of *kein-*.

210. Wir haben leider ————— Zeit.

211. Sie gibt es ————— anderen Frau.

212. Das gehört ————— anderen Kind.

213. ————— von euch ist heute hier.

In the following "word-search" puzzle there are ten interrogative and indefinite pronouns. Try to find them.

214.

A	C	D	R	W	E	G	S
B	K	L	W	E	M	L	T
J	E	M	A	N	D	O	N
R	I	A	S	E	T	S	A
A	N	N	I	C	H	T	S
O	W	E	S	S	E	N	E
P	E	T	N	L	G	Z	T
R	L	W	E	R	I	N	E
K	R	A	N	T	O	P	S
S	O	S	E	L	N	S	E

3.
ERBS

Fill in the correct present-tense forms of the verbs in parentheses.

215. Warum _____ du das? *(tun)*

216. Georg _____ die Antwort. *(wissen)*

217. Karl _____ nach Hause. *(laufen)*

218. Paul _____ den ganzen Tag. *(arbeiten)*

219. Anna _____ die Zeitung. *(lesen)*

220. Er _____ das Auto. *(waschen)*

221. Wie _____ du? *(heißen)*

222. Was _____ du da? *(essen)*

223. Warum _____ er ihm Geld? *(geben)*

224. Warum _____ du ihn nicht? *(grüßen)*

225. Ich _____ zufrieden. *(sein)*

226. Wir _____ zu Hause. *(sein)*

227. Er _____ ein Auto. *(haben)*

228. Ihr _____ ein Haus. *(haben)*

229. Du _____ Arzt. *(werden)*

Fill in the correct past-tense forms of the verbs in parentheses.

230. _____ du es ihr? *(sagen)*

231. Gestern _____ wir sehr viel. *(arbeiten)*

232. Sie _____ unser Spiel. *(filmen)*

233. Er _____ den Baum. *(zeichnen)*

234. Ihr _____ das Fenster. *(öffnen)*

Fill in the correct past-tense forms of the irregular verbs in parentheses.

235. Er _____ mir ein Buch. *(bringen)*

236. Die Schule _____ nieder. *(brennen)*

237. Er _____ den Mann. *(nennen)*

238. Wir _____ nach Hause. *(rennen)*

239. Alfred _____ den Sänger. *(kennen)*

240. Paul _____ ihr Blumen. *(senden)*

Fill in the correct past-tense forms of the auxiliary verbs in parentheses.

241. Gestern _____ sie im Theater. *(sein)*

242. _____ du genug? *(haben)*

243. Er _____ viel Geld. *(haben)*

244. Was _____ sie? *(werden)*

Fill in the correct present perfect forms of the verbs in parentheses.

> EXAMPLE:
> *Er _____ einen Wagen _____. (kaufen)*
> *Er hat einen Wagen gekauft.*

245. Sie _____ den ganzen Tag _____. *(arbeite*

246. Karl, _____ du die Wahrheit _____? *(sage*

247. Wir _____ die Tür _____. *(öffnen)*

248. Ich _____ in Frankfurt _____. *(wohnen)*

249. _____ ihr das _____? *(glauben)*

250. _____ du mit ihm _____ ? *(telefonieren)*

251. Wir _____ die Karten _____. *(bestellen)*

252. Karl, _____ du dein Haus _____? *(verkaufe*

253. Wem _____ das Auto _____? *(gehören)*

Fill in the correct present perfect forms of the auxiliary verbs in parentheses.

> EXAMPLE:
> *Er _____ in der Schule _____. (sein)*
> *Er ist in der Schule gewesen.*

254. _____ du im Kino _____? *(sein)*

255. _____ er Fieber _____? *(haben)*

256. Wir _____ Besuch _____. *(haben)*

257. Mein Freund _____ Arzt _____. *(werden)*

Rewrite the following sentences, using the past tense.

> EXAMPLE:
> *Ich fahre nach Wien. Ich fuhr nach Wien.*

258. Er spricht mit mir. _____

259. Sie trifft mich heute. —————————.

260. Wir sitzen auf der Bank. —————————.

261. Sie schwimmt im Fluß. —————————.

262. Singst du das Lied? —————————?

263. Trinkt ihr Bier? —————————?

264. Er schläft den ganzen Tag. —————————.

265. Wir laufen zehn Kilometer. —————————.

266. Sie liest ein Drama. —————————.

267. Bleibst du zu Hause? —————————?

Form sentences from the following, using the present perfect tense.

> EXAMPLE:
> *Er / sehen / den Mann   Er hat den Mann gesehen.*

268. Er / die Flasche / brechen —————————.

269. Sie / das Geld / stehlen —————————.

270. Du / ihn / treffen? —————————?

271. Wir / die Frau / bitten —————————.

272. Ich / viel Geld / gewinnen —————————.

273. Er mich / schlagen —————————.

274. Sie / die Bluse / waschen —————————.

275. Wir / an ihn / denken. —————————.

276. Ich / dir etwas / bringen —————————.

277. Das / ich / wissen —————————.

Choose the correct auxiliary verb in the following sentences.

> EXAMPLE:
> *Er hat / ist / nach Hause gefahren. ist*

278. Peter hat / ist / auf den Baum geklettert. —————

279. Hast du / bist du / heute geschwommen? —————

280. Mein Freund hat / ist / heute erschienen. (appeared)
—————

281. Seine Frau ist / hat / heute gekommen. —————

282. Wir haben / wir sind / zu Hause geblieben. —————

283. Sie hat / ist / viel gelesen. _____

Rewrite the following sentences in the past perfect tense.

EXAMPLES:
Wir haben studiert. Wir hatten studiert.
Ich bin gegangen. Ich war gegangen.

284. Habt ihr sie gefragt? _____

285. Ich habe viel getrunken. _____

286. Er hat mich besucht. _____

287. Wann ist er gekommen? _____

288. Wir sind in New York gewesen. _____

Complete the following sentences by using the future tense of the verbs in parentheses.

EXAMPLE:
Ich _____ das Buch (lesen).
Ich werde das Buch lesen.

289. _____ du die Tür *(öffnen)?*

290. Sie _____ den Brief *(schreiben).*

291. _____ ihr ihn *(anrufen)?*

292. Wir _____ morgen in Berlin *(sein).*

Complete the following by using the familiar forms of the imperative in the singular.

EXAMPLE:
_____ schnell! (kommen) Komm *schnell!*

293. _____ weniger! *(sprechen)*

294. _____ gut! *(schlafen)*

295. _____ das Geld! *(nehmen)*

296. _____ den Kuchen! *(essen)*

297. _____ bald! *(schreiben)*

Rewrite the following commands, changing the singular familiar to the plural familiar.

EXAMPLE:
Lies das Buch! Lest das Buch!

298. Gib mir die Zeitung! _____

299. Sprich zu mir! _____!

300. Nimm den Mantel! _____!

301. Sei nicht dumm! _____!

Form sentences changing the verbs to the present and the past subjunctive.

> EXAMPLES:
> *Ich schreibe dir gern.*
> *Ich schriebe dir gern. Ich hätte dir gern geschrieben.*

302. Er kommt vielleicht. _____ . _____ .

303. Wir wissen das nicht. _____ . _____ .

304. Er sagt mir, sie denken an dich. Er sagt mir,
_____ . Er sagt mir, _____ .

305. Er sagt, er hat Zahnweh. (toothache) Er sagt,
_____ . Er sagt, _____ .

306. Frau Schmidt behauptet (maintains), er ist zu Hause.
Frau Schmidt behauptet, _____ . Frau Schmidt
behauptet, _____ .

Complete the following by using the correct present subjunctive form of the verb indicated.

> EXAMPLE:
> *Wenn ich hier _____, _____ ich Ihnen (sein, helfen).*
> *Wenn ich hier <u>wäre</u>, <u>würde</u> ich Ihnen helfen.*

307. Wenn er Geld _____ , würde er es uns *(haben, geben)*.

308. Wenn ich es _____ , würde ich es euch *(wissen, sagen)*.

309. Wenn Sie jetzt _____ , würden wir Karten *(gehen, spielen)*

310. Wenn wir reich _____ , würden wir ein Haus *(sein, kaufen)*

311. Wenn du den Wein _____ , würde ich ihn *(bestellen, trinken)*.

Here is a little story with missing verbs. Fill in the correct German form(s) of the verbs in parentheses.

312. Die Lehrerin ＿＿＿＿＿ (spoke) zu ihren Schülern: „＿＿＿＿＿ (write) eine kurze Geschichte: Was ＿＿＿＿＿ (would) ich tun, wenn ich zehn Millionen Mark ＿＿＿＿＿ (had)?"
Jeder Schüler ＿＿＿＿＿ (began) sofort zu schreiben, nur Michael nicht. Nach einer halben Stunde ＿＿＿＿＿ (gave) Michael der Lehrerin ein leeres Blatt.
„Was ist das, Michael?" ＿＿＿＿＿ (asked) ihn die Lehrerin. „Jeder andere Schüler ＿＿＿＿＿ (wrote) zwei Seiten oder mehr."
„Frau Lehrerin," ＿＿＿＿＿ (replied) Michael. „Das ist es, was ich ＿＿＿＿＿ (would do), wenn ich ein Millionär ＿＿＿＿＿ (would be)."

Form sentences from the following words, using the present tense of the verb and the appropriate form of the adjective or article.

EXAMPLE:
Das Buch / gehören / mein / Tante   Das Buch gehört meiner Tante.

313. Er / helfen / sein / Bruder ＿＿＿＿＿＿＿＿＿

314. Sie / antworten / ihr / Lehrerin ＿＿＿＿＿＿＿

315. Danken / du / dein / Freund? ＿＿＿＿＿＿＿

316. Ich / glauben / das / Kind ＿＿＿＿＿＿＿＿

Insert the appropriate reflexive verbs and pronouns in the present tense.

317. Wir ＿＿＿＿＿ ＿＿＿＿＿ vor ihm. *(sich fürchten)*

318. Ich ＿＿＿＿＿ ＿＿＿＿＿ nach ihr. *(sich sehnen)*

319. Er ＿＿＿＿＿ ＿＿＿＿＿ langsam von seiner Krankheit. *(sich erholen)*

320. ＿＿＿＿＿ ＿＿＿＿＿ den Kopf! *(sich waschen, singular familiar)*

Fill in the correct past tense of the verbs in parentheses.

EXAMPLE:
Er ＿＿＿＿＿ heute ＿＿＿＿＿. (ausgehen)
Er ging heute aus.

321. Edith ＿＿＿＿＿ die Arbeit ＿＿＿＿＿. *(anfangen)*

322. Wir _____ ihn auf die Reise _____ . *(mitnehmen)*

323. Kurt _____ uns für heute _____ . *(einladen)*

324. Anna _____diesmal auch _____ . *(mitfahren)*

325. Er _____ die Tür _____ . *(zumachen)*

Fill in the correct present perfect tense of the verbs in parentheses.

EXAMPLE:
Er _____ die Prüfung _____ . (bestehen)
Er hat die Prüfung bestanden.

326. Erika _____ eine Violine _____ . *(bekommen)*

327. _____ du das Bild _____ ? *(verkaufen)*

328. Wir _____ die Antwort _____ . *(verstehen)*

329. Wer _____ Amerika _____ ? *(entdecken)*

Fill in the proper form of the modal verbs (in parentheses) in the present tense.

330. _____ er mitkommen? *(können)*

331. _____ du rauchen? *(dürfen)*

332. _____ ihr nach Hause gehen? *(müssen)*

333. _____ Sie es sehen? *(wollen)*

334. _____ du die Zeitung? *(mögen)*

Rewrite the following, using the proper form of the modal verb.

EXAMPLE:
Er studiert viel. (müssen)
Er muß viel studieren.

335. Sie kommt nach Wien. *(sollen)* _____ .

336. Paul arbeitet heute. *(können)* _____ .

337. Er ißt Kuchen. *(dürfen)* _____ .

338. Ich helfe ihm. *(müssen)* _____ .

Rewrite the following sentences in the present perfect tense.

EXAMPLE:
Wir konnten nicht kommen. Wir haben nicht kommen können.

339. Er konnte nicht lesen. _____ .

340. Sie wollte ihm schreiben. _____

341. Karl durfte nicht rauchen. _____

342. Ich mußte viel studieren. _____

343. Wir mochten heute nicht ausgehen. _____

Rewrite the following sentences in the future tense.

EXAMPLE:
Ich muß mir das Auto kaufen.
Ich werde mir das Auto kaufen müssen.

344. Er kann es nicht tun. _____

345. Ich will ihn sehen. _____

346. Sie darf keine Schokolade essen. _____

347. Er mag Franz nicht sehen. _____

348. Mußt du nach Wien fahren? _____

Change the following sentences (in the present tense) from the active to the passive voice.

EXAMPLES:
Herr Müller baut ein Haus.
Das Haus wird von Herrn Müller gebaut.
Die Ärztin hilft dem Kranken.
Dem Kranken wird von der Ärztin geholfen.

349. Die Mutter bringt das Frühstück. _____

350. Der Mechaniker repariert den Fernseher. _____

351. Wasser ruiniert (ruins) die Bücher. _____

352. Frau Schmidt wäscht die Kleider. _____

353. Er dankt mir für das Geschenk (gift). _____

Change the following sentences (past tense, present perfect) from the active to the passive voice.

EXAMPLES:
Bomben verwüsteten (devastated) das Land.
Das Land wurde durch Bomben verwüstet.
Dr. Braun hat Fritz behandelt.
Fritz ist von Dr. Braun behandelt worden.

354. Franz parkte das Auto.
     Das Auto _____ _____ Franz _____.

355. Feuer zerstörte das Haus.
     Das Haus _____ _____ Feuer _____.

356. Die Lehrerin half dem Jungen.
Dem Jungen _____ _____ der Lehrerin
_____ .

357. Karl hat die Rechnung bezahlt.
Die Rechnung _____ _____ Karl _____
_____ .

358. Ich habe dem Mädchen einen Brief geschrieben.
Dem Mädchen ist _____ _____ ein Brief
_____ _____ .

In the word-search puzzle below, try to find the correct past-tense forms (third person singular) of the following strong German verbs: *bitten, blasen, fangen, gehen, heben, liegen, schlagen, sterben, tragen, treffen*

359.

S	T	A	R	B	O	E	S
E	R	B	L	A	G	L	M
R	A	L	O	T	R	U	G
A	F	I	N	G	D	S	I
E	Z	E	A	N	E	T	N
B	A	S	C	H	L	U	G
A	G	A	B	O	R	L	E
D	E	L	B	B	O	N	T

§9.
ADVERBS

Fill in the German equivalents of the English adverbs in parentheses.

360. Ich hoffe, er kommt _____ zurück. (soon)

361. _____ ist es wärmer als gestern. (today)

362. Das Problem ist _____ schwer. (rather)

363. Wir warteten sehr lange, aber _____ kam er. (finally)

364. Er hatte leider nicht _____ zu essen. (enough)

Fill in the German equivalents of the English adverbs in parentheses.

365. Das ist _____ der Rede wert. (hardly)

366. Er ist _____ gestorben. (almost)

367. Frau Schmidt war _____ hier. (already)

368. _____ wußte er nichts davon. (probably)

369. Sie hatte _____ viel Geld. (allegedly)

370. Ich kann ihm _____ helfen. (possibly)

Choose the sentences in which the adverb *gern* is positioned correctly.

371.
Gern ich schwimme.	☐
Er hat ihn sehr gern.	☐
Dir wir gern helfen.	☐
Gern er macht es.	☐
Wir haben ihn gern getroffen.	☐

Choose (from the list) the best German equivalents of the English adverbs in parentheses, and insert them in the following sentences.

also, erst, noch, nur, wohl

372. Er ist _____ krank. (probably)

373. Sie hat _____ Zeit. (still)

374. Sie soll es _____ wissen! (by all means)

375. Er ist _____ fünf Jahre alt. (only)

376. _____ ist er endlich fertig? (well)

§10. PREPOSITIONS

Rewrite the following sentences, using the correct prepositional contractions.

EXAMPLE:
Komm in das Haus! Komm ins Haus!

377. Er geht zu der Schule. _____

378. Sie bekommt es von dem Lehrer. _____

379. Paul steht an dem Fenster. _____

380. Er ist in dem Zimmer _____

Choose the correct prepositions from the list below, and insert them in the sentences that follow.

bei, bis, für, gegen, gegenüber, nach, seit, um, während, wegen.

381. Sie geht _____ die Ecke.

382. Er wohnt _____ ihm.

383. Wir warten _____ acht Uhr.

384. Ich kenne ihn _____ fünf Jahren.

385. Die Schule ist der Bank _____.

386. Es gibt _____ zwanzig Kinos in der Stadt.

387. Sie kam _____ des Abends.

388. _____ dem Mittagessen gingen wir aus.

389. _____ der Kälte trug sie einen Mantel.

390. Er arbeitet _____ seinen Vater.

Some prepositions take the dative or the accusative.
Underline the correct version in each pair of sentences.

391. Setz dich neben ihn!
     Setz dich neben ihm!

392. Leg das Buch auf den Tisch!
     Leg das Buch auf dem Tisch!

393. Wirf das Heft unter dem Sessel!
     Wirf das Heft unter den Sessel!

394. Er steht hinter das Haus.
     Er steht hinter dem Haus.

395. Sie geht in der Schule.
     Sie geht in die Schule.

Insert the correct prepositions from the list below.

an, aus, für, mit, vor

396. Er hat Angst _____ ihr.

397. Wir sind _____ guter Musik interessiert.

398. Sie hat eine Vorliebe _____ große Ohrringe.

399. Ich habe Mitleid _____ dem Kind.

400. Das Armband besteht _____ Holz und Kupfer.

11. CONJUNC- TIONS

Fill in the German equivalents of the English conjunctions.

401. Du bleibst zu Hause, _____ ich muß ausgehen. (but)

402. Hans ist _____ dumm _____ faul. (either – or)

403. Wir gehen ins Theater _____ ins Kino. (or)

404. Das Kind ist brav _____ fleißig. (and)

405. Wir gehen nicht in den Park, _____ ins Museum. (but)

406. Er spricht _____ Spanisch _____ Französisch. (neither—nor)

Fill in the correct conjunctions from the list below.

als, als ob, bevor, bis, so daß, wenn.

407. Er wartet, _____ ich nach Hause komme.

408. Peter rasiert sich, _____ er ausgeht.

409. Sie sieht mich an, _____ _____ ich chinesisch redete.

410. Hilde wusch das Geschirr, _____ sie zurückkam.

411. Bitte ruf mich an, _____ du Zeit hast.

412. Es regnete die ganze Woche, _____ _____ man nicht Fußball spielen konnte.

Combine the simple sentences below, forming complex sentences by using the subordinating conjunctions in the parentheses.

EXAMPLE:
Es war sehr kalt. Wir waren in Kanada. (als)
Es war sehr kalt, als wir in Kanada waren.

413. Sie konnte nicht ausgehen. Sie war krank. *(weil)* _____
_____ .

414. Ich weiß. Sie hat eine Katze. *(daß)* _____

415. Er kann nicht gut schlafen. Er hatte den Unfall. *(seitdem)* _____

§12. WORD FORMATION

Give the correct gender of the compound nouns below by filling in the appropriate definite article *(der, die, das).*

416. _____ Teilnehmerverzeichnis (telephone directory), _____ Kohlenbergbau (coal-mining industry), _____ Flugzeugfabrik, _____ Geburtstagskuchen, _____ Lichtspieltheater (movie theater)

Choose the correct form of the compound noun in the sets below.

417.
Lieblingbuch ☐
Lieblingsbuch ☐

418.
Universitätsprofessor ☐
Universitätprofessor ☐

419. The noun prefix *Miß-* indicates
nothing important ☐
a synonym ☐
an opposite ☐

420. The prefix *Ur-* can indicate
origin ☐
an opposite ☐
a timepiece ☐

421. The prefix *Rück-* indicates
going back ☐
starting out ☐
continuing ☐

422. The prefix *ver-* indicates the action of a verb that is mostly
positive ☐
negative ☐
indifferent ☐

423. The prefix *zer-* denotes the action of a verb that is
constructive ☐
neutral ☐
destructive ☐

424. Nouns with the suffixes *-ei, -heit, -keit, -schaft, -ung, -ion,* and *-tät,* are always
masculine ☐
feminine ☐
neuter ☐

425. Nouns with the suffixes *-chen* and *-lein* are always
masculine ☐
feminine ☐
neuter ☐

§13. COMMON PHRASES AND IDIOMATIC EXPRESSIONS

Give the English meaning of the following idiomatic expressions.

426. Er kauft auf Zeit. _____

427. Er hat Geld wie Heu. _____

428. Sie geht in die Luft. _____

429. Er kommt auf keinen grünen Zweig. _____

430. Das sitzt ihm wie angegossen. _____

431. Es steht nicht dafür. _____

432. Sie hat Grütze im Kopf. _____

§14. NUMBERS

Which of the three German numbers is written correctly?

433.
372,875 ☐
372.875 ☐
372 875 ☐

How do you pronounce the number 501 in German?

434.
fünfhunderteins ☐
fünfhundertundeins ☐
fünfhundertein ☐

Which of the sentences below is correct?

435.
Ich traf ein oder zwei Freunde. ☐
Ich traf einen oder zwei Freunde. ☐
Ich traf eine oder zwei Freunde. ☐

Which would be the correct German equivalent of *the 12th*

436.
12 ☐
12. ☐
12te ☐

How do you pronounce "May 9" in German?

437.
der neunte Mai ☐
Mai der neunte ☐
Mai neunter ☐

Which is the correct version?

438.
Das kostet drei Mark und fünfzig. ☐
Das kostet drei fünfzig Mark. ☐
Das kostet drei Mark fünfzig. ☐

A billion in the United States is equivalent to which of the following?

439.   eine deutsche Billion   ☐
                                 eine deutsche Milliarde ☐
                                 eine deutsche Trillion   ☐

§15.
TELLING TIME

Write in German the time shown on each of the following clocks. Use the twenty-four-hour system, the German *Bahnzeit*.

440. Wie spät ist es?

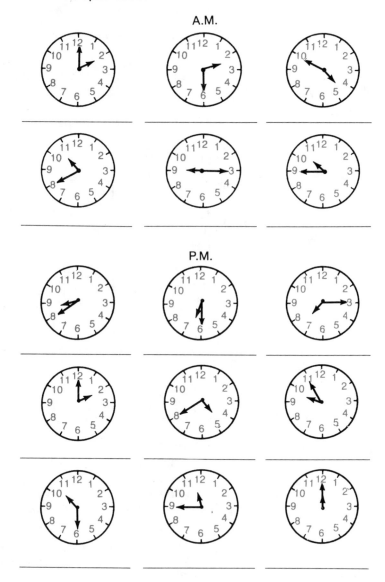

A.M.

P.M.

§16.
DAYS,
MONTHS,
SEASONS,
DATES, AND
THE
WEATHER

In which city do many people say *Sonnabend* instead of *Samstag*?

441.   Berlin   ☐
                                          Vienna ☐
                                          Munich ☐

Which is the correct way of dating a German letter?

442.   18. August 1986 ☐
                              August 18, 1986 ☐
                              8/18/86   ☐

Which sentence is *incorrect*?

443.   Er wurde 1850 geboren.   ☐
                Er wurde im Jahre 1850 geboren. ☐
                Er wurde in 1850 geboren.   ☐

Fill in German words that have to do with months, dates, and the weather.

444.

N							
O							
V							
E							
M							
B							
E							
R							

fog
month
forecast
icy
month
dreadful cold
our planet
rain

§17.
SYNONYMS
AND
ANTONYMS

Match the synonyms.

445. wieder   albern
      sonderbar   erwidern
      entzückend   nochmals
      gestatten   wahrnehmen
      antworten   seltsam
      entsetzlich   reizend
      beobachten   erlauben
      dumm   abscheulich
      wirklich   nun
      jetzt   tatsächlich

Fill in the appropriate forms of either *wissen* or *kennen*.

446. Er _____, daß du recht hast.

447. _____ Sie meinen Bruder?

448. Er _____ dieses Lied.

449. _____ Sie, wann er nach Hause kommt?

Match the antonyms.

450. die Frage   der Friede (n)
     billig   schnell
     lachen   verlieren
     langsam   die Antwort
     der Krieg   teuer
     finden   weinen
     der Tag   krank
     gesund   die Nacht
     viel   reich
     arm   wenig

Answers

§1. PRONUNCIA-TION

1–10 (see §1.2 and §1.3)

1. vain
2. tsar
3. fine
4. lure
5. boy
6. *sht*
7. *ks*
8. mailed
9. mouse
10. *ü*
11. (see §1.4) der <u>Gar</u>tenstuhl, ge<u>gan</u>gen, stu<u>die</u>ren, Brauer<u>ei</u>

§2. ORTHOG-RAPHY

12, 13 (see §2.1)

12. Freund, Zeit, Nase, die Neun, das Schwimmen, Präsident

13. das Alte, etwas Kleines

14, 15 (see §2.2)

14. Ansichts-karte

15. Bäk-ker

16–23 (see §2.3)

16. Königin Elisabeth II.

17. Fritz trank Kaffee, und Edith trank Tee.

18. Er glaubt, daß du recht hast.

19. Wenn du zurückkommst, gehen wir ins Kino.

20. Ich weiß nicht, ob ich das tun kann.

21. Ich reise nach Italien, Spanien und Frankreich.

22. Er kaufte sich ein Hemd, einen Schlips und Schuhe.

23. Ich werde heute ins Kino gehen!

§3.
WORD ORDER

24 – 32 (see §3.1)

24. Karl arbeitet mit ihr im Wohnzimmer.

25. Er erzählt dem Mädchen die Geschichte.

26. Paul ging vor einer Stunde ins Büro.

27. Natürlich gehen wir aus.

28. Gestern kam er zurück.

29. Morgen fährt er mit.

30. Ihrem Bruder will sie helfen.

31. Den Vater werde ich sehen.

32. Auf ihn mußte ich warten.

33, 34 (see §3.2 – 1)

33. Ich gebe dem Vater ein Buch.

34. Ich kaufe der Tante ein Geschenk.

35 – 37 (see §3.2 – 2)

35. Er hat heute nicht studiert.

36. Fritz arbeitete heute leider nicht.

37. Nicht sie, sondern er spielt heute Bridge.

38 – 40 (see §3.2 – 3)

38. Warum öffnen Sie die Tür?

39. Wieviel hat das Sofa gekostet?

40. Wann kommt er?

41 – 44 (see §3.3 – 2)

41. Das Mädchen, das den Ball wirft, ist meine Schwester.

42. Bevor du ins Kino gehst, mußt du mir helfen.

43. Weil ich kein Geld habe, kann ich nichts kaufen.

44. Ich lese weniger, seit du hier bist.

§4.
NOUNS

45 – 54 (see §4.2 – 1)

45. das

46. die

47. das

48. der

49. die

50. das

51. der

52. das

53. der

54. die

55. (see §4.3) das, der, die, die, die

56–60 (see §4.4–1)

56. Jungen

57. Frau

58. Arztes

59. Kind

60. Vater

61–73 (see §4.4–2)

61. Mädchen

62. Löffel

63. Äpfel

64. Lehrern

65. Briefe

66. Häuser

67. Gläser

68. Männern

69. Zeitungen

70. Türen

71. Tassen

72. Radios

73. Sofas

74–78 (see §4.4–3 and 4.4–4)

74. Namen

75. Herzen

76. Themen

77. Rhythmen

78. Museen

79.

Autos
Hotels
Kameras
Parks

P	A	R	K	S	T	L	H	K
M	O	N	A	W	I	N	O	M
K	A	M	M	E	M	D	T	S
O	P	Z	E	R	D	T	E	R
A	L	G	R	O	N	A	L	A
G	B	Z	A	U	T	O	S	N
A	B	O	S	L	I	N	G	T

80–82 (see §4.5)

80. Vaters

81. Frankreichs

82. Londons

§5.
ARTICLES

83–87 (see §5.2)

83. Der Tod ist unvermeidlich.

84. Die Natur ist sehr schön.

85. Wir haben Geduld.

86. Der Ätna ist in Sizilien.

87. Heute ist der 5. April.

88–91 (see §5.3)

88. Ich bin Spanier.

89. Sie wird Lehrerin.

90. Wir fragten ihn als Fachmann.

91. Er hat Temperatur.

92–96 (see 5.4)

  92. das, dieses

  93. den, diesen

  94. dem, diesem

  95. dies

  96. jene

97–106 (review §5.2, 5.3, and 5.4)

  97. der

  98. einem

  99. des

100. die

101. diesem

102. eine

103. den

104. diesen

105. eines

106. dieses

§6.
ADJECTIVES

107–115 (see §6.1–1)

107. guten

108. schöne

109. blonden

110. alten

111. neue

112. netten

113. kleinen

114. neue

115. alten

116–122 (see §6.1–2)

116. Guter

117. Schönes

118. alte

119. andere

120. kleine

121. großes

122. Frische

123 – 127 (see §6.1 – 3)

123. gute

124. neuen

125. altes

126. alten

127. neuen

128 – 132 (see §6.1 – 4)

128. Kleinen

129. Alte

130. Blonde

131. Bekannter

132. Gutes

133 – 139 (see §6.2 – 1 and 6.2 – 2)

133. gesünder, gesündeste, gesündesten

134. ärmer, ärmsten, ärmsten

135. höher, höchste, höchsten

136. besser, beste, besten

137. mehr, meisten

138. wie

139. als

§7.
PRONOUNS

140 – 148 (see §7.1 – 1)

140. du

141. Er

142. es

143. Sie

144. Ich

145. ihr

146. wir

147. Sie

148. Sie

149 – 157 (see §7.1 – 2)

149. ihn

150. sie

151. es

152. dich

153. mich

154. sie

155. euch

156. uns

157. Sie

158 – 166 (see §7.1 – 2)

158. mir

159. dir (Ihnen)

160. ihr

161. ihm

162. ihm

163. ihnen

164. uns

165. euch (Ihnen)

166. Ihnen

167 – 173 (see 7.1 – 3)

167. mich

168. uns

169. dich

170. mir

171. dir

172. sich

173. einander

174 – 180 (see §7.2)

174. Sein

175. unsere

176. Ihr

177. meines

178. euer

179. ihrem

180. Ihre

181 – 183 (see §7.2)

181. deinen

182. deines

183. sein, dein

184 – 193 (see §7.3)

184. dem

185. den

186. der

187. das

188. das

189. der

190. dessen

191. deren

192. die

193. denen

194 – 200 (see §7.4)

194. Wer wohnt in München?

195. Wessen Mantel ist das?

196. Wem gehört der Ball?

197. Wen sieht Albert?

198. Was spielen sie?

199. Welches Auto gefällt ihm?

200. Welcher Mann ist am größten?

201–204 (see §7.4)

201. Woran arbeitet er?

202. Wovon redet sie?

203. Worüber lachst du?

204. Wofür braucht er es?

205–209 (see §7.5)

205. niemand

206. etwas

207. man

208. nichts

209. alle

210–213 (see §7.5)

210. keine

211. keiner

212. keinem

213. Keiner

214.

etwas
jemand
kein
man
nichts
was
wem
wen
wer
wessen

A	C	D	R	W	E	G	S
B	K	L	W	E	M	L	T
J	E	M	A	N	D	O	N
R	I	A	S	E	T	S	A
A	N	N	I	C	H	T	S
O	W	E	S	S	E	N	E
P	E	T	N	L	G	Z	T
R	L	W	E	R	I	N	E
K	R	A	N	T	O	P	S
S	O	S	E	L	N	S	E

8.
ERBS

215–229 (see §8.2–1)

215. tust

216. weiß

217. läuft

218. arbeitet

219. liest

220. wäscht

221. heißt

222. ißt

223. gibt

224. grüßt

225. bin

226. sind

227. hat

228. habt

229. wirst

230–234 (see §8.2–2)

230. sagtest

231. arbeiteten

232. filmten

233. zeichnete

234. öffnetet

235–240 (see §8.2–2)

235. brachte

236. brannte

237. nannte

238. rannten

239. kannte

240. sandte (sendete)

241 – 244 (see §8.2 – 2)

241. war (waren)

242. Hattest

243. hatte

244. wurde (wurden)

245 – 253 (see §8.2 – 3)

245. hat (haben)/ gearbeitet

246. hast / gesagt

247. haben / geöffnet

248. habe / gewohnt

249. Habt / geglaubt

250. Hast / telefoniert

251. haben / bestellt

252. hast / verkauft

253. hat / gehört

254 – 257 (see §8.2 – 3)

254. Bist / gewesen

255. Hat / gehabt

256. haben / gehabt

257. ist / geworden

258 – 267 (see §8.2 – 2 and §8.2 – 3)

258. Er sprach mit mir.

259. Sie traf mich heute.

260. Wir saßen auf der Bank.

261. Sie schwamm im Fluß.

262. Sangst du das Lied?

263. Trankt ihr Bier?

264. Er schlief den ganzen Tag.

265. Wir liefen zehn Kilometer.

266. Sie las ein Drama.

267. Bliebst du zu Hause?

268–277 (see §8.2–3)

268. Er hat die Flasche gebrochen.

269. Sie hat das Geld gestohlen.

270. Hast du ihn getroffen?

271. Wir haben die Frau gebeten.

272. Ich habe viel Geld gewonnen.

273. Er hat mich geschlagen.

274. Sie hat die Bluse gewaschen.

275. Wir haben an ihn gedacht.

276. Ich habe dir etwas gebracht.

277. Das habe ich gewußt.

278–283 (see §8.2–3)

278. ist

279. Bist du

280. ist

281. ist

282. Wir sind

283. hat

284–288 (see §8.2–4)

284. Hattet ihr sie gefragt?

285. Ich hatte viel getrunken.

286. Er hatte mich besucht.

287. Wann war er gekommen?

288. Wir waren in New York gewesen.

289–292 (see §8.2–5)

289. Wirst du die Tür öffnen?

290. Sie werden (wird) den Brief schreiben.

291. Werdet ihr ihn anrufen?

292. Wir werden morgen in Berlin sein.

293–297 (see §8.3)

293. Sprich weniger!

294. Schlaf gut!

295. Nimm das Geld!

296. Iß den Kuchen!

297. Schreib bald!

298–301 (see §8.3)

298. Gebt mir die Zeitung!

299. Sprecht zu mir!

300. Nehmt den Mantel!

301. Seid nicht dumm!

302–306 (see §8.4)

302. Er käme vielleicht. Er wäre vielleicht gekommen.

303. Wir wüßten das nicht. Wir hätten das nicht gewußt.

304. Er sagt mir, sie dächten an dich. Er sagt mir, sie hätten an dich gedacht.

305. Er sagt, er hätte Zahnweh. Er sagt, er hätte Zahnweh gehabt.

306. Frau Schmidt behauptet, er wäre zu Hause. Frau Schmidt behauptet, er wäre zu Hause gewesen.

307–311 (see §8.5)

307. Wenn er Geld hätte, würde er es uns geben.

308. Wenn ich es wüßte, würde ich es euch sagen.

309. Wenn Sie jetzt gingen, würden wir Karten spielen.

310. Wenn wir reich wären, würden wir ein Haus kaufen.

311. Wenn du den Wein bestelltest, würde ich ihn trinken.

312. sprach   Schreibt   würde   hätte
     begann   gab   fragte   schrieb
     antwortete   tun würde   wäre

313–316 (see §8.6–2)

313. Er hilft seinem Bruder.

314. Sie antwortet (antworten) ihrer Lehrerin.

315. Dankst du deinem Freund?

316. Ich glaube dem Kind.

317–320 (see §8.6–3)

317. fürchten uns

318. sehne mich

319. erholt sich

320. Wasch dir

321–325 (see §8.6–4)

321. Edith fing die Arbeit an.

322. Wir nahmen ihn auf die Reise mit.

323. Kurt lud uns für heute ein.

324. Anna fuhr diesmal auch mit.

325. Er machte die Tür zu.

326–329 (see §8.6–5)

326. Erika hat eine Violine bekommen.

327. Hast du das Bild verkauft?

328. Wir haben die Antwort verstanden.

329. Wer hat Amerika entdeckt?

330–334 (see §8.8)

330. Kann

331. Darfst

332. Müßt

333. Wollen

334. Magst

335–338 (see §8.8)

335. Sie soll nach Wien kommen.

336. Paul kann heute arbeiten.

337. Er darf Kuchen essen.

338. Ich muß ihm helfen.

339–343 (see §8.8)

339. Er hat nicht lesen können.

340. Sie hat ihm schreiben wollen.

341. Karl hat nicht rauchen dürfen.

342. Ich habe viel studieren müssen.

343. Wir haben heute nicht ausgehen mögen.

344–348 (see §8.8)

344. Er wird es nicht tun können.

345. Ich werde ihn sehen wollen.

346. Sie wird keine Schokolade essen dürfen.

347. Er wird Franz nicht sehen mögen.

348. Wirst du nach Wien fahren müssen?

349–353 (see §8.9–1)

349. Das Frühstück wird von der Mutter gebracht.

350. Der Fernseher wird von dem (vom) Mechaniker repariert.

351. Die Bücher werden durch Wasser ruiniert.

352. Die Kleider werden von Frau Schmidt gewaschen.

353. Mir wird von ihm für das Geschenk gedankt.

354–368 (see §8.9–2 and §8.9–3)

354. Das Auto wurde von Fritz geparkt.

355. Das Haus wurde durch Feuer zerstört.

356. Dem Jungen wurde von der Lehrerin geholfen.

357. Die Rechnung ist von Karl bezahlt worden.

358. Dem Mädchen ist von mir ein Brief geschrieben worden.

359.

S	T	A	R	B	O	E	S
E	R	B	L	A	G	L	M
R	A	L	O	T	R	U	G
A	F	I	N	G	D	S	I
E	Z	E	A	N	E	T	N
B	A	S	C	H	L	U	G
A	G	A	B	O	R	L	E
D	E	L	B	B	O	N	T

bat
blies
fing
ging
hob
lag
schlug
starb
trug
traf

9.
DVERBS

360–364 (see §9.1, §9.2, and §9.3)

360. bald

361. Heute

362. ziemlich

363. schließlich

364. genug

365–370 (see §9.3, §9.4, and §9.5)

365. kaum

366. beinahe

367. bereits (schon)

368. Wahrscheinlich

369. angeblich

370. möglicherweise

371. (see §9.6) Er hat ihn sehr gern.
Wir haben ihn gern getroffen.

372–376 (see §9.7)

372. wohl

373. noch

374. nur

375. erst

376. Also

§10. PREPOSITIONS

377–380 (see §10.1)

377. Er geht zur Schule.

378. Sie bekommt es vom Lehrer.

379. Paul steht am Fenster.

380. Er ist im Zimmer.

381–390 (see §10.2–1, §10.2–2, and §10.2–4)

381. um

382. bei

383. bis

384. seit

385. gegenüber

386. gegen

387. während

388. Nach

389. Wegen

390. für

391–395 (see §10.2–3)

391. Setz dich neben ihn!

392. Leg das Buch auf den Tisch!

393. Wirf das Heft unter den Sessel!

394. Er steht hinter dem Haus.

395. Sie geht in die Schule.

396–400 (review the chapter)

396. vor

397. an

398. für

399. mit

400. aus

11. CONJUNC-TIONS

401–406 (see §11.1)

401. aber

402. entweder, oder

403. oder

404. und

405. sondern

406. weder, noch

407–412 (see §11.2)

407. bis

408. bevor

409. als ob

410. als

411. wenn

412. so daß

413–415 (see §11.2)

413. Sie konnte nicht ausgehen, weil sie krank war.

414. Ich weiß, daß sie eine Katze hat.

415. Er kann nicht gut schlafen, seitdem er den Unfall hatte.

12. WORD FORMATION

416–418 (see §12.1)

416. das, der, die, der, das

417. Lieblingsbuch

418. Universitätsprofessor

419–425 (see §12.2 and §12.3)

419. an opposite

420. origin

421. going back

422. negative

423. destructive

424. feminine

425. neuter

§13.
COMMON PHRASES AND IDIOMATIC EXPRESSIONS

426–432 (see §13.1 and §13.2)

426. He buys on credit.

427. He is loaded.

428. She flies into a rage.

429. He'll never make the grade.

430. It fits him like a glove.

431. It is not worth it.

432. She has brains.

§14.
NUMBERS

433. 372 875

434. fünfhunderteins

435. Ich traf ein oder zwei Freunde.

436. 12.

437. der neunte Mai

438. Das kostet drei Mark fünfzig.

439. eine deutsche Milliarde

§15.
TELLING TIME

440. Es ist zwei Uhr.
Es ist zwei Uhr dreißig. Es ist halb drei.
Es ist vier Uhr fünfzig. Es ist zehn Minuten vor fünf.
Es ist zehn Uhr vierzig. Es ist zwanzig vor elf.
Es ist neun Uhr fünfzehn. Es ist fünfzehn nach neun.
Es ist zehn Uhr fünfundvierzig. Es ist dreiviertel elf.
Es ist zwanzig Uhr vierzig. (20:40)
Es ist achtzehn Uhr dreißig. (18:30)
Es ist neunzehn Uhr fünfzehn. (19:15)
Es ist vierzehn Uhr. (14:00)
Es ist sechzehn Uhr vierzig. (16:40)
Es ist einundzwanzig Uhr fünfundfünfzig. (21:55)
Es ist zwanzig Uhr dreißig. (20:30)
Es ist dreiundzwanzig Uhr fünfundvierzig. (23:45)
Es ist vierundzwanzig Uhr. Es ist Mitternacht. (24:00)

16.
AYS,
ONTHS,
EASONS,
ATES, AND
HE WEATHER

441. Berlin

442. 18. August 1986

443. Er wurde in 1850 geboren.

444.

N	E	B	E	L				
O	K	T	O	B	E	R		
V	O	R	A	U	S	S	A	G	E
E	I	S	I	G				
M	A	I						
B	Ä	R	E	N	K	Ä	L	T	E
E	R	D	E					
R	E	G	E	N				

17.
YNONYMS
ND
NTONYMS

445. (see §17.1)

wieder	nochmals
sonderbar	seltsam
entzückend	reizend
gestatten	erlauben
antworten	erwidern
entsetzlich	abscheulich
beobachten	wahrnehmen
dumm	albern
wirklich	tatsächlich
jetzt	nun

446–449 (see §17.1)

446. weiß

447. Kennen

448. kennt

449. Wissen

450. (see §17.2)

die Frage	die Antwort
billig	teuer
lachen	weinen
langsam	schnell
der Krieg	der Friede(n)
finden	verlieren
der Tag	die Nacht
gesund	krank
viel	wenig
arm	reich

Index

References in this index are to the Brush-Up section (consisting of the Basics, the Parts of Speech, and Special Topics) indicated by the symbol § (section) followed by a number. References to Verb Charts, Test Yourself and Let's Review are given by page (pp.) number.

NOTES

NOTES

NOTES

NOTES

NOTES